YOUR FREEDOM, YOUR POWER

YOUR FREEDOM, YOUR POWER

★ A KID'S GUIDE TO THE ★
FIRST AMENDMENT

ALLISON MATULLI

with Clelia Castro-Malaspina

Illustrated by
CARMELLE KENDALL

RP|KIDS
PHILADELPHIA

Running Press Kids
Hachette Book Group
1290 Avenue of the Americas, New York, NY 10104
www.runningpress.com/rpkids
@RP_Kids

Printed in Malaysia

First Edition: July 2023

Published by Running Press Kids, an imprint of Perseus Books, LLC, a subsidiary of Hachette Book Group, Inc. The Running Press Kids name and logo are trademarks of the Hachette Book Group.

The Hachette Speakers Bureau provides a wide range of authors for speaking events. To find out more, go to www.hachettespeakersbureau.com or email HachetteSpeakers@hbgusa.com.

Running Press books may be purchased in bulk for business, educational, or promotional use. For more information, please contact your local bookseller or the Hachette Book Group Special Markets Department at Special.Markets@hbgusa.com.

The publisher is not responsible for websites (or their content) that are not owned by the publisher.

Print book cover and interior design by Marissa Raybuck and Frances J. Soo Ping Chow.

Library of Congress Control Number: 2022920562

ISBNs: 978-0-7624-7838-5 (hardcover), 978-0-7624-7839-2 (ebook)

PCF

10 9 8 7 6 5 4 3 2 1

PHOTO CREDITS:
AP Photo/James A. Finley © p 95;
BJC (Baptist Joint Committee for Religious Liberty) © p 34;
Pete Souza © p 155; Getty Photos © pp 11, 29, 40, 47, 59, 128, 131, 138, 151, 165;
National Child Labor Committee collection, Library of Congress, Prints and Photographs Division © p 125

To my mother, Adelene, who came to America with twenty dollars in her purse and unlimited bravery to construct a path forward with endless opportunities in this powerful nation. She inspires me each and every day to believe in human greatness and my own talent to change the world.

—A. M.

To my parents, Agnes and Hugo, for inspiring my law career and always supporting me.

—C. C. M.

Contents

INTRODUCTION

The First Amendment of the United States is something all people, even kids, may need, want, or have to use at some point in their lives. But even if you've heard about it, maybe you're not sure exactly what it is or what it means. The First Amendment is present in so many parts of kids' lives—it's present in the words you say, the clothes you wear, the religion you practice, the posts you read and write on social media, the places you get your information, the causes you care about, the rules your school enforces, and more! If the First Amendment is everywhere, shouldn't you know more about it? The answer is YES! The First Amendment guarantees you—and every other citizen in the United States—five monster freedoms: freedom of religion, freedom of speech, freedom of the press, freedom of assembly, and the right to petition the government. That's right: these freedoms are *yours*, so now it's time to understand just how they work.

In this book, you will get to know just how the First Amendment affects your life—right now—as a kid. You'll also be introduced to real kids who have fought to protect their own First Amendment rights. These kids are amazing for many reasons, but especially for the fact that they knew enough about these rights to fight for them when they seemed at risk of losing them! As for me, I didn't even really learn about my own First Amendment rights until I was an adult. I was twenty-two and a law student on the campus of Howard University School of Law, a historically Black university known for creating the leaders of the Civil Rights Movement and a legacy of legal minds who fight for equality. At that time, I knew that I had these things called rights that protected me and that were packed into a really important paper called the Constitution, but I had little to no idea about all the details of those rights. I began to wonder why I hadn't learned more about my rights as a kid. It's strange when you think about how we spend thousands of hours in school, thousands more at friends' houses, on sports fields, at parties, in doctors' offices, on vacations, and with our family, but, on average, maybe only a few hours in life learning all the rights and laws meant to protect us in all of those places.

The goal for this book is to give you the special power that comes with knowing your own rights. Wouldn't I have liked to feel this way as a kid? Wouldn't knowing more about my rights have helped me better understand the world around me? Maybe it would have even helped me see trouble coming from a mile away. Or inspired me to stir up some "good trouble," as civil rights activist John Lewis once said. Law is in every action, interaction, and reaction. It's time that you know how to identify all the positive ways you can use the law to make a better world for you, your local community, and the universe. You gotta fight for your rights to understand your true power!

—**ALLISON MATULLI,**
founder of The Little Lawyers

YOUR FREEDOM,
YOUR POWER

The Constitution and the Bill of Rights

Creating a Country from Scratch:
The Making of the Constitution

You've probably heard of the US Constitution. You may know just what it is—but maybe all you know is that it's important. You know it means a lot to Americans. You know that it was created by some famous old white guys a long time ago. Maybe you even know that it's a document that starts with "We the People . . ." It *is* all of those things—and so much more.

The Constitution is the single most important piece of writing in American history. In just four pages of handwritten parchment paper, it sets up the entire framework for how we create and run our government. The Constitution, plus the twenty-seven amendments that came later, is considered the "supreme law of the land." Every single American is affected by the Constitution, from families who have been here for generations to newly arrived immigrants; from Democrats to Republicans; from great-grandmas and -grandpas to kids just like you. The Constitution is for everyone.

In the summer of 1787, the United States of America was still brand new. If countries were people, it was just an infant in diapers—it had been only eleven years since the Declaration of Independence announced to the world that the United States was breaking free from British rule to become its own country. This baby version of the USA still had no real set form of government. Essentially, the thirteen original states were operating as their own mini countries rather than one unified country, each with their own constitutions. Every state, attempting to thrive on its own, was trying to figure out how to keep its citizens safe and happy, while safeguarding its government from corruption and creating laws that made sense for its own population. It's important to remember that not all the states were equal when they were created. That means they didn't have the same size, agriculture, land, or number of people. And these thirteen baby states operated independently of each other, meaning they had only the limited resources contained within their state lines. Governing was really tough stuff and hard to get right! So, many of their leaders thought: *Wouldn't it be better if we joined forces?*

It was time to create a centralized, or federal, government—a strong one. A government that would act as a parental figure, one that could live on forever and withstand wars, good or bad presidents, natural disasters, market meltdowns, and any other curveball history threw at it. This was really unusual. A group of men was coming together to figure out how to set up a country completely from scratch. Much of the world watched with interest. There was a lot of pressure to succeed.

The first step was to organize a gathering—a party of sorts. But not the kind where you barbecue hamburgers and hot dogs; it was the kind where important figures from across the states gathered together to share their ideas and debate their differences until they all came to an agreement. Since they couldn't Zoom in for this historic meeting of the minds, each state sent delegates—spokespersons or elected officials—to the biggest city in the country at the time—Philadelphia, Pennsylvania—to represent its state interests.

The event was called the Constitutional Convention, and the delegates were among the who's who from the upper crust of white, landowning men.

Women—wealthy or not—were not invited to be delegates because, at the time, politics was not considered an appropriate activity for women to participate in. How times have changed! The delegates included some very famous people whose names you've heard of: George Washington, Benjamin Franklin, James Madison, and Alexander Hamilton. You know, the guys who appear on dollar bills and coins, who have been memorialized in giant statues, and who have had important buildings or even a smashingly successful Broadway musical named after them.

States Represented in the Constitutional Convention of 1787

CONNECTICUT	NEW JERSEY
DELAWARE	NEW YORK
GEORGIA	NORTH CAROLINA
MARYLAND	PENNSYLVANIA
MASSACHUSETTS	SOUTH CAROLINA
NEW HAMPSHIRE	VIRGINIA

Isn't that only twelve states? Weren't there thirteen original states? Good eye! Rhode Island sent no delegates. It boycotted the Constitutional Convention because it did not like the idea of a powerful national government. It was the last original state to ratify the Constitution in 1790.

There were fifty-five delegates in all, ranging from age twenty-six to eighty-one. The eighty-one-year-old was Benjamin Franklin, who was in such bad physical condition because of his age that he had to be carried to work every day. The convention lasted one hundred hot, sweaty summer days, with the delegates enclosed in an un-air-conditioned hall, debating all day, every day about every single word to include on each line of the Constitution. Now you know how Benjamin Franklin's dedication earned him a place not only in American history but also on the crispy one-hundred-dollar bill.

The language used would shape the life of each and every citizen in this newly founded nation. The pressure was monumental. The delegates knew they had to get it right!

The drafters of the Constitution were figuring out answers to fundamental questions. We're not talking questions about how often officials must powder their wigs or whether the tricornered hat should be the official headgear of the country. No, their discussion topics centered on one theme: How will this great new American experiment be different from the oppression and restrictions under British rule?

Getting everyone to agree was really hard. All the states had different interests, opinions, and ideas based on what was important to their citizens. The delegates debated each point thoroughly. Arriving at a final version of the document took an enormous amount of time and compromise from everyone.

Some of the important ideas delegates to the Constitutional Convention debated and eventually incorporated into the Constitution include the following:

★ There are three branches of government: legislative, executive, and judicial.

★ Two groups of elected representatives from each state are in charge of making federal laws: the Senate and the House of Representatives.

★ Each state sends two senators to represent its interests in the Senate.

★ Each state elects its number of congresspeople to represent its interests in the House of Representatives on the basis of its population.

★ A president elected by the people is the leader of the country.

★ An elected president has to be at least thirty-five years old and a natural-born citizen.

★ The president's powers include being head of the military and the leader of executive agencies; the ability to pardon people who have committed crimes; the ability to make treaties with foreign countries; and the ability to sign bills into law or to veto bills (say no to them).

★ A vice president is second in command and votes in the Senate if there is a tie.

★ The Supreme Court is the most powerful court in the country and has the final say on legal cases.

★ The Supreme Court is made up of a group of justices who can serve life terms.

★ Amendments to the Constitution can be made with approval from two-thirds of the Senate and two-thirds of the House of Representatives.

★ Each state has the right to pass its own laws.

★ State laws should not conflict with federal laws.

After one hundred days, they finally finished their work. On September 17, 1787, the delegates attending the Constitutional Convention signed the Constitution. Nine out of the thirteen states had to ratify the Constitution for it to pass. Five states—Delaware, Pennsylvania, New Jersey, Georgia, and Connecticut—ratified right away, one after the other. However, the other states hesitated because the Constitution, at that very moment, failed to afford citizens everyday protections or basic rights, such as freedom of religion, speech, and the press. Once an agreement was made that amendments, or changes, to the Constitution would be immediately proposed, Massachusetts, Maryland, and South Carolina ratified it. New Hampshire was lucky number nine when it ratified the Constitution on June 21, 1788. From then on, the Constitution was officially the supreme law of the land. And America officially had its government. The same one we have today, nearly 250 years later.

Adding the Bill of Rights

Creating the Constitution was an incredible accomplishment—but the Constitution wasn't perfect. It wasn't perfect at all! In the decades following its ratification, fixing the Constitution ignited politicians, legal scholars, and average Americans to keep pushing for changes. Let's explore the most pressing changes made.

First of all, the original Constitution didn't give the same rights to all citizens. It allowed for states to give voting rights only to white men who owned property. Think about who that left out: all women, all Black and Indigenous people, and men who were too poor or incapable of owning property.

Second, it didn't put a stop to slavery. The newly minted United States had an opportunity to end this cruel and inhumane practice, and it didn't. Instead, the Constitution's language allowed for slavery, the forced labor

and ownership of enslaved Black people, to continue for nearly eighty more years. Slavery was an effective bargaining chip used by the delegates from the southern states, who did not agree to sign the Constitution unless slavery was allowed. Even delegates who were strongly opposed to slavery caved on this point, because they decided creating the Constitution was the most important thing to do right then—even though it came at a very steep human cost. In what's called the Three-Fifths Clause, only three-fifths of enslaved people were counted toward the population for representation and taxation purposes. Although this was agreed upon for political reasons, the message was clear: enslaved people were not considered equal to the rest of Americans. It was decades before the Constitution was amended and laws were passed to grant enslaved people and their ancestors equal rights.

Making History

THREE-FIFTHS A PERSON?

The Three-Fifths Compromise gives us a window into the deep feud between North and South, free and enslaved, abolitionists and slaveholders. It was all about "the count." Delegates at the Constitutional Convention decided that the bigger the population of a state, the more representatives and electoral votes that state would have to influence the federal government. So, of course, southern states wanted their enslaved population to be included in "the count." Counting them as part of the population would boost their numbers big time and, thus, their influence. Even though southern states weren't interested in giving enslaved people any rights. Northern delegates, some of whom were abolitionists who wanted an end to the cruel practice of slavery, did not want enslaved people to be included in "the count." By law, they were not allowed to vote, so it didn't seem fair to the northern delegates that southern states would get more power and influence through representation based on a population that couldn't participate in an election. If the South was willing to make its enslaved population free men and women, that may have changed the conversation—but that option wasn't even on the table. The whole thing was a mess, and the two sides fought hard to advance their ideas. **This resulted in the Three-Fifths Compromise, which you can read directly in the Constitution today:**

> Representatives and direct Taxes shall be apportioned among the several States which may be included within this Union, according to their respective Numbers, which shall be determined by adding to the whole Number of free Persons, including those bound to Service for a Term of Years, and excluding Indians not taxed, three fifths of all other Persons.

The "other Persons" were enslaved people. Each state's number of representatives and amount of taxation were originally based on population, which did not count enslaved Black people and American Indians as full human beings. Can you picture what three-fifths of a person looks like? No one can. Or telling someone that their existence doesn't matter because they are merely three-fifths of a human being? Well, that's what happened. By the end of the convention and compromise, the North and South threads were joined together into the Union, but their struggle to stay tied had only just begun. The law fractioning human beings into three-fifths of a person was finally changed in section 2 of the Fourteenth Amendment, which was adopted to the Constitution on July 9, 1868—almost ninety years later!

Both of these major flaws of the Constitution were remedied over time, but a third major flaw was dealt with almost right away by the newly created Congress. The Constitution laid out all the things that the government had the power to do, but it didn't set up any protections for citizens against abuses of that power. People from every state were interested in adding a bill of rights to the Constitution. Not the kind of bill you get at a restaurant or from a shop, but a formal list of rights guaranteed to citizens to protect them from a government that behaves completely bonkers or unfairly. Why was this a top priority to loads of people? Because so many of the first Americans came here to get away from overly powerful governments that treated them unjustly. No one wanted a replay of the unfair treatment they or their ancestors had faced.

When the Bill of Rights was passed in 1791, it became a federal law, meaning it was applicable to the US government. But what about individual states—could their governments make laws that differed from the Bill of Rights? It wasn't until 1868 that a new amendment to the Constitution, the Fourteenth one to be exact, made clear that the Bill of Rights was the law for both the federal government and all state governments. This is referred to as the "incorporation doctrine."

Many states had already laid out citizens' rights in their state constitutions. Virginia was really ahead of the game and had its very own bill of rights. Even England, the country many had fled from, had the Magna Carta, a document of rights that shielded its citizens from abuses of power by the monarchy, or their royal leader. The inspirations were there, so the question was—who was going to write this thing? The man for the job was James Madison, then a congressman from Virginia, who would eventually become the fourth president of the United States.

Known for his tiny five-foot-four-inch frame, and weighing just about a hundred pounds, James Madison was small but mighty—his intellect delivered a bill of rights that would impact the rest of American history. After he finished writing his draft, Madison spent the next two and a half years pushing, persuading, even pestering his fellow congressmen to finally accept it. Today, we call this type of ongoing convincing *lobbying*! Eventually, states agreed to ten of his proposed rights, and each is known as an amendment—or a change—to the Constitution. The Bill of Rights, the first ten amendments to the Constitution, was officially ratified and made into law on December 15, 1791. Without James Madison and his can't-stop-won't-stop American spirit, we wouldn't have the Bill of Rights as we know it today.

James Madison

What We're All Here For: The First Amendment

That finally brings us to the First Amendment—and the epic reason you're here reading this book. The First Amendment is FIRST for a reason. The freedoms it protects are considered of the utmost importance to the American people. It guarantees not just one freedom, but five! Americans hold each of these freedoms close; they are essential to the core of the American identity and spirit. Creating a country from scratch, the founders tried their best to make it as perfect as possible—an ideal country. These freedoms were critical to the vision of that ideal. In many ways, the First

Amendment is as American as apple pie. And guess what? All Americans are welcome to a slice of that delicious pie!

So, what does it say?

Here is the First Amendment, in all of its glory:

> **Congress shall make no law respecting an establishment of religion, or prohibiting the free exercise thereof; or abridging the freedom of speech, or of the press; or the right of the people peaceably to assemble, and to petition the government for a redress of grievances.**

This amendment was going in the Constitution, after all, so it had to be stated all fancy. In regular-person speak, the First Amendment ensures Americans keep the following rights:

Freedom of religion o Freedom of speech
Freedom of the press o Freedom of assembly
Freedom to petition (aka ask the government for change)

These five rights are for everyone—including kids. Yes! You read that right: kids have rights too! Since the day these freedoms were promised to Americans, kids have been using them and also pushing back when they've felt like these rights were being taken away or were at risk. In fact, kids have been at the center of some of the most hard-fought legal battles and inspiring social movements in history.

Before We Dive In: The US Federal Court System

When you think of the American court system, you probably think of it as crawling with grown-ups—judges, lawyers, jurors, people in stuffy suits walking around in lavish buildings and seriously rigid courtrooms. It seems to be a world strictly for adults. But American history is chock-full of court cases involving kids. Some kids have taken their battle from the classroom to the courtroom. They've filed lawsuits to fight against injustices and to stand up for themselves.

But before we dive into the fascinating history of some of these First Amendment cases, it's a good idea to go over some basics about the US court system and how it works.

Is the First Amendment Federal Law or State Law?

There are two primary, separate court systems in the United States—the state court system and the federal court system, although tribal courts and military courts also exist. In this book, we discuss only cases in the federal system. You may rightfully ask, "Why is that?" At the heart of all of the legal disagreements we discuss is the First Amendment, a law from the US Constitution—which is federal (not state) law. The federal court system is the right place, or jurisdiction, for disagreements about federal laws like the First Amendment to be decided.

LEGAL LINGO

FEDERAL Related to the national government as opposed to state governments.

JURISDICTION In the United States, there are many different courts. Courts divide the cases among themselves by subject matter and geography. This power to accept certain kinds of cases and make legal decisions and judgments is called jurisdiction.

The First Amendment is a mere forty-five words written a whopping 250 years ago. Can it cover everything? Can it solve every free speech problem? Does it resolve each petition made or protest started? In a word—NO! In two—absolutely not! You see, it was written in really general and broad terms. When disagreements over, say, free speech happen, they usually involve lots of facts and circumstances that make it hard to answer for sure whether the First Amendment was violated or not. The founders couldn't have written the First Amendment in a way that accounts for every single

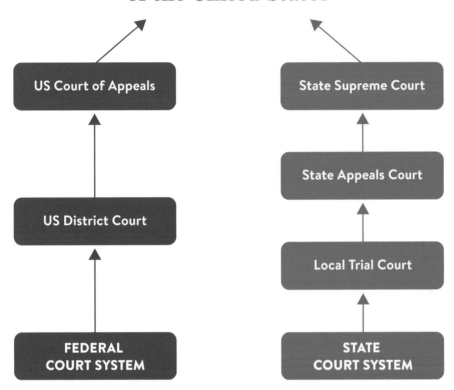

Supreme Court of the United States

US Court of Appeals

State Supreme Court

State Appeals Court

US District Court

Local Trial Court

FEDERAL COURT SYSTEM

STATE COURT SYSTEM

situation—it's impossible to do that. They also had no ability to see into the future and how things like cultural norms and technology would evolve and how the words would apply in those situations.

So, that's where the courts come in. Whether or not things seem black and white or just plain foggy gray, the courts go over all of the facts and circumstances to figure out which ones violate the First Amendment and which ones don't. When a court makes a decision, it becomes the law. If a similar or the same situation arises later involving new people (or *parties*, as they are called in legal cases) after one case has already been decided by the courts, everyone then has a better idea whether the First Amendment was violated.

A Road Trip to the Supreme Court

Alright, now it's time to go on a trip to the Supreme Court of the United States. The Supreme Court is so well known that it has its own nickname. Picture an acronym using the first letter of each word of the official name and, voilà—SCOTUS! From here on out, we'll call our friend, the highest court in the land, SCOTUS.

When someone decides to pay a visit to SCOTUS, the reason for the trip is to resolve a disagreement. For example, you believe someone has denied you one of your First Amendment rights. But the person who you think is responsible for denying your rights thinks they were acting in a totally fine way. So, you file a lawsuit, which means you ask a court to formally rule that this party or person did you wrong. Last, and most important, you want the court to also make things right.

Let's think of this as a journey or real road trip. You're going to fill your car up with passengers before you get started. As the person who files the lawsuit, you're the **plaintiff**, and you're the driver. Your first passenger is your lawyer, who is going to help you navigate or find the right road—or the laws to prove your point. Unfortunately, you aren't too fond of another passenger in your car—it's the person you're mad at. The **defendant**, along with their lawyer, is coming along with you for this ride. That's right! Each path or step your case takes through the courts, you and the defendant are going to be on the same road—together.

Now that all the passengers are buckled in—the plaintiff, the defendant, the lawyers—all armed with reading material (their legal arguments), it's time for the first stop: **US District Court**.

Federal district courts decide cases that happen in a region of the country. Sometimes the region is an entire state or, for big states, just a part of it. District court is also called trial court, and it's the kind of court you're probably most familiar with. The kind you've seen on TV or in movies. There's a judge in a robe, lawyers making arguments, and sometimes, witnesses being questioned and evidence being presented in trials.

After both parties, plaintiff and defendant, have argued their side of their First Amendment case, there is the final decision on the matter called an **opinion**. In the opinion, the judge gives all of his or her reasons for making this final decision after evaluating all the facts and circumstances in the case and looking at the law as well as previous relevant cases and what other judges have said in similar situations. In most cases, the judge decides either for the plaintiff or for the defendant—there is a winner and a loser. At this point, the party who won is super happy, and the party who lost is feeling downright upset. Even though the party who won might want to call this journey quits and head on home, it's not necessarily the end. The losing party has the ability to add another stop to this trip—the **US Court of Appeals**.

Either party—the winner or the loser (although it's usually the loser)—has the right to file an appeal, or ask a higher court "Can you look this over,

and if possible, change the decision? Pretty please!" The party, or person, who appeals is called the **appellant**. When they appeal the district court's decision, the appellant is hoping that the court of appeals will think that the district court made a mistake or was just plain wrong, that the case can be reconsidered, and that the case can be decided in the appellant's favor. The court of appeals is called a "higher" court because it has the right to over-turn—cancel—the district court's opinion. The court of appeals also has the right to alter parts of the district court's ruling or even to tell the district court to rehear the case entirely, starting the legal process over.

In the federal court system, a court of appeals is also known as a cir-cuit court. Circuit courts cover an even bigger geographic area than district

CIRCUIT COURTS OF APPEALS

DC: DC Circuit

1: First Circuit: Maine, Massachusetts, New Hampshire, Rhode Island, Puerto Rico

2: Second Circuit: Connecticut, New York, Vermont

3: Third Circuit: Delaware, New Jersey, Pennsylvania, US Virgin Islands

4: Fourth Circuit: Maryland, North Carolina, South Carolina, Virginia, West Virginia

5: Fifth Circuit: Louisiana, Mississippi, Texas

6: Sixth Circuit: Kentucky, Michigan, Ohio, Tennessee

7: Seventh Circuit: Illinois, Indiana, Wisconsin

8: Eighth Circuit: Arkansas, Iowa, Montana, Minnesota, Missouri, Nebraska, North Dakota, South Dakota

9: Ninth Circuit: Alaska, Arizona, California, Guam, Hawaii, Idaho, Montana, Nevada, Oregon, Washington

10: Tenth Circuit: Colorado, Kansas, New Mexico, Oklahoma, Utah, Wyoming

11: Eleventh Circuit: Alabama, Georgia, Florida

Fed: Federal Circuit and Supreme Court: Washington, DC

courts and, often, multiple judges will hear a single case so that decisions are made by a panel of judges instead of just one. This time, in the court of appeals, there's no trial. Judges review the arguments the lawyers already made in the district court. Just like judges in district courts, when the circuit court judges come to a decision, they issue their opinion explaining their reasoning.

Once again, there is a winner and a loser. Sometimes, the winner is the same winner of the district court case—they can now be doubly sure the law is on their side. Other times, the winner is the loser from the district court case, and this party is feeling pretty darn good about their come-from-behind victory.

Does this mark the end of the trip? Not necessarily. There's one more possible stop. The losing party at this stage may want to appeal the circuit court decision to an even *higher* court. This is their last hope, and this destination requires a ticket. Not everyone gets in. At this point, we call the person who is appealing the **petitioner** because they are petitioning—asking—SCOTUS to review their case.

It's really, really tough to convince SCOTUS to take a case. Things that are easier: getting into Harvard, catching a foul ball at a baseball game, and convincing your parents to replace that video game console you broke! Every year, thousands of petitioners send in a petition, but only a handful are chosen. On average, about 3 percent of potential cases are reviewed by the SCOTUS justices. To decide to take on a case, SCOTUS must think it represents a crucial issue. Sometimes, different lower circuit courts issue contrary opinions on cases that deal with the same legal issue and even similar facts. So then, in one state, a certain behavior is allowed and lawful, but if you take a trip to your grandma's across the country, that same behavior is illegal. Where there is this type of confusion and inconsistency, SCOTUS justices want to give their final word and settle the differences of opinions on important matters.

If your case has been accepted by SCOTUS—congratulations! You are headed to a very beautiful destination that few have had the right to travel to! The Supreme Court is located in a stately marble building in Washington, DC. Lawyers give oral arguments in front of the nine justices. While the lawyers argue their cases, the justices interrupt them with lots of questions, trying to poke holes in their reasoning and understand their arguments. It's very nerve-wracking!

In the end, the justices finally issue their opinion, and that opinion is the final word on the issue, officially the law of the land. This time, it's winner takes all, which means your legal case has reached the end of its journey.

What's So Supreme
About the Supreme Court?

SCOTUS existed shortly after the United States formally existed. The founders established it and its importance in Article III of the Constitution. The judicial branch is one of the three branches of government, along with the executive and legislative branches. SCOTUS sits at the top of the judicial branch.

Nine justices review every case for SCOTUS. The president of the United States appoints justices to the court, and the Senate confirms their appointment. Once you get the job of Supreme Court justice, it's yours for life! That's right, you have it till your last breath—unless you decide to retire or you get kicked out for bad behavior. Justice Oliver Wendell Holmes was the oldest justice who sat on the Supreme Court bench—he was ninety years old when he retired in 1932.

The Supreme Court is supreme because it gets the last word on legal cases, and its decisions are the most important legal decisions of all.

Legal Opinions

Once a legal opinion is issued by a district court, not only does it decide that particular case but also other courts in the same district have to follow it. When the circuit court issues an opinion, all the lower district courts located in that circuit's region have to follow that decision. When the Supreme Court issues an opinion, *all* courts across the country have to follow it.

3 Freedom of Religion

> **Congress shall make no law respecting an establishment of religion, or prohibiting the free exercise thereof . . .**

In its first sixteen words, the First Amendment guarantees two very BIG things:

1. The government can't establish an official national religion.

2. The government can't interfere with peoples' religious beliefs and practices.

America is a religious country—but we don't have a religious government. How did that happen? By design, of course!

Religion has always been a powerful force in our nation. The Founding Fathers chose to cement religious freedom—that is, the freedom of all to exercise whatever religion they choose—as the very first freedom. It's listed even before freedom of speech.

Why?

They'd seen for themselves what happens when a government doesn't accept all religions. Many of America's first colonists were people who fled their home country, leaving absolutely everything behind, just to start brand new lives. Sound drastic? It was!

Why would anyone do that?

It's simple. They dreamed of practicing their faith freely. It may sound extreme or even unheard of, especially if you've grown up always having religious freedom. But back then, countless people lived in total fear of punishment or judgment or outright hatred just because of their religion. Today, America is one of the most religious of the developed nations in the world. Even among our younger generations, Americans consider themselves religious. A whopping two-thirds of American teens practice a religion.

Religious Symbols Around Us

More than half of teens see other students wearing religious clothing (like a headscarf or turban) or jewelry with religious symbols (like a Jewish Star of David or Christian cross necklace) at school. Count how many people around you in class, at camp, after school, or on your sports team are wearing some type of religious object. Did you expect to see as many as you did?

But what if you find yourself thinking, "This doesn't matter to me because I'm not religious!"? You're not alone. Not everyone is religious or follows a religion. And, guess what? The First Amendment protects people who are nonreligious, too. The government can't interfere with those who choose not to practice religion either.

Another reason religious freedom matters is because religion influences things that are happening all around us. The intensely personal nature of religion makes people feel really passionate about many things. And, in fact, some people have their BIGGEST differences of opinions deeply rooted in or influenced by religion.

Like what?

For example, in recent years Americans have found themselves in courtrooms arguing about the following:

- o If or when the right to abortion should be allowed at certain times during pregnancy or never at all
- o Whether a baker can decline making a wedding cake for a same-sex couple
- o If a transgender boy or girl can use the same bathroom as boys and girls identifying with their gender at birth
- o When and where vaccines can be mandatory, especially if someone states that their religion doesn't support it

The Government's Important Promises About Religion

We call the first promise of religious freedom the Establishment Clause. Have you ever made a major promise to someone about something super important? Well, the Establishment Clause is the government's important promise to you—its citizen—about religious fairness. Under it, the government can't favor a religion and it can't give its official stamp of approval to one religion over others. The government must remain neutral and unbiased. Not only is the government not allowed to name an official religion, it also can't make anyone attend religious services or force anyone to pray or partake in any kind of religious act. Everyone is free to make their own decisions about how to practice—or not practice—religion. Now that's a major promise!

Under the Establishment Clause, the government and all the institutions that extend from it—like public schools—must always be secular, aka nonreligious. This idea is often referred to as the "separation of church and state." Think of a wall built in between matters of the government and mat-ters of the church (or temple, mosque, gurdwara, synagogue, or shrine). The goal of this separation is to make sure no one feels like an outsider in their own country because of their religion—that every citizen is an equal and full member of the American community.

Now, the second promise, the best buddy of the Establishment Clause, is called the Free Exercise Clause: Americans are free to believe in and worship whatever religion they want. People should never be punished for expressing themselves religiously, and they shouldn't be prevented from doing so, as well.

With its opening Establishment Clause and Free Exercise Clause, the First Amendment makes a bold statement: we are a country of religious tolerance.

The Founding of American Religious Freedom

Many of the colonists who fled their home countries because of religious persecution came from England. England had a history of establishing an official religion. But it wasn't always the same religion. It became problematic for people whenever the ruler changed—because so could the official religion. One day a person of one religion could be a law-abiding citizen, and the next day they were breaking the law by attending their church services.

Not only was this confusing, it was downright scary. People who were not a member of the officially approved religion could be punished, could be made into social outcasts, or could be on the receiving end of hatefulness and bigotry. Some brave souls decided they'd rather start over somewhere new and departed for the land that lay across the Atlantic Ocean. You'd guess that these colonists had learned their lesson and would work really hard to establish a new home that was open-minded and tolerant about religion? Not quite. Actually, not at all.

By the time the American Revolution kicked off, eight of the thirteen former colonies had declared official religions—all sects of Christianity. Mistreatment of those who weren't practicing the established religion was common. Some nonbelievers were even put in jail, fined, or had their children taken away from them because they were deemed "unfit parents." This bad sequel to England's religious persecution taught us an important lesson: hatred, disrespect, and intolerance were pretty much a given when a government officially favored one religion over others. And Thomas Jefferson, James Madison, and other founders were going to have none of that in their newly formed United States of America. Even though many of these men were religious themselves, they strongly believed that government-established religion and religious persecution went hand-in-hand. America must be a country of religious tolerance. The words they drafted in the First Amendment cemented that deeply held belief and hope.

LIMITS ON RELIGIOUS FREEDOM

Just like all of the other freedoms in the First Amendment, freedom of religion isn't limitless. In certain situations, the government can create a law or act in a certain way that affects someone's religious practice or worship. Think of one of those old-timey scales that weigh two different things. On one side is the weight of religious freedom. It's super important, so it's a very heavy weight. We're talking elephant-who-ate-three-helpings-of-dinner kind of weight. For the government to be allowed to place a limit on religious freedom, it has to show a "compelling interest," aka a really, really good reason. The weight of the government's reason on the other side of the scale has to be even heavier than the weight of religious freedom. An elephant-who-ate-ten-helpings kind of weight! That's a tough thing to do.

Let's take a real-life example. The custom in Amish families is to withdraw their kids from school after the eighth grade, when children are thirteen or fourteen years old. But a state law requires kids have to go to school until they're sixteen. Does the First Amendment protect the Amish families and allow them to take their kids out of school early? Let's first weigh the elephant that is religious freedom. Here, it takes the form of the fact that Amish people strongly believe that higher education could corrupt their children's Christian values. As an agricultural community, they also need members of their families to start working at an early age. In short, to Amish people, keeping kids in school after the eighth grade goes against their religion.

On the other side of the scale is the government's interest. This is a big elephant, too: education is important and we know it's good for kids to go to school until at least the age of sixteen. In the end, SCOTUS decided that forcing Amish families to go against their religion in this way was wrong, so the scale was tipped in their favor. As a result, Amish families are allowed to pull their kids from school after the eighth grade.

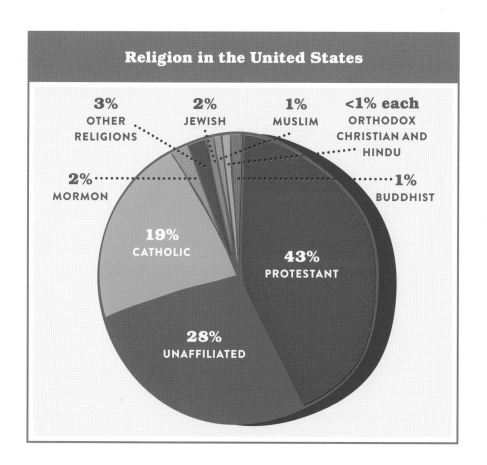

Religion in the United States

- **3%** OTHER RELIGIONS
- **2%** JEWISH
- **1%** MUSLIM
- **<1% each** ORTHODOX CHRISTIAN AND HINDU
- **2%** MORMON
- **1%** BUDDHIST
- **19%** CATHOLIC
- **43%** PROTESTANT
- **28%** UNAFFILIATED

Public Schools and Prayer

Prayer is one of the most important and personal expressions of religion. To many people, prayer happens daily and it's a part of their regular life. Fifty-five percent of Americans say they pray every day! Others may save prayer for when they are in their house of worship or when they are most in need of divine support. And others don't pray at all—perhaps they don't believe in God. The US government respects all of these decisions about prayer by keeping prayer out of public schools. With so many different opinions about the importance of prayer, it's not surprising there's been a lot of disagreement about this. Courts in the United States have looked at the issue of prayer in school many times over and over again.

PRAYER IN THE CLASSROOM

In 1951, the Hyde Park, New York, school district announced a new requirement. Every morning, a twenty-two-word prayer had to be read aloud to all the students in the district, from elementary school on up to high school. The prayer stated:

> *Almighty God, we acknowledge our dependence upon Thee, and we beg Thy blessings upon us, our parents, our teachers and our Country.*

The Hyde Park community was mostly made up of practicing Christians, with a growing Jewish community. The prayer, called the "Regents' Prayer," had actually been written for the state by a team of ministers, priests, and rabbis. It was purposefully nondenominational, meaning it didn't reflect any specific religion's beliefs. But while a lot of religions believe in God or a higher power, other religions don't. Buddhism doesn't recognize a supreme god, Hinduism recognizes more than one god, and Muslims refer to their supreme power as "Allah." And atheists don't believe in any god. Several students and their parents weren't happy about the school's required prayer. Not only did it force prayer on students who might have been uncomfortable with it, those in opposition believed the school shouldn't be in the business of requiring any student prayer. The angry parents said it was the role of the parent, not the school, to educate their children about religion. Others said such a watered-down version of a prayer took away the meaning of prayer, which was supposed to be a special thing.

Fifty families filed a lawsuit, called *Engel v. Vitale*, believing the prayer violated the First Amendment and was unconstitutional. At first, they had strength in numbers, but by the time the trial came about, only five families were left. Their cause had proven really unpopular in their mostly Christian community and they were subject to major bullying. Many of the families who dropped out of the case had had enough and weren't even sure if the courts would rule in their favor.

In 1962, the case arrived before SCOTUS, and the justices weren't impressed with the Regents' Prayer or the Hyde Park School Board. By requiring a prayer, the public school system was endorsing religion. It didn't matter that it tried to be nondenominational or that the students had the choice to say it themselves or not—it was a school-approved religious activity and it violated the First Amendment.

This was a really important case because it was the first time the highest court in the country officially said: **public school–sponsored prayer is not okay**. A lot of people were really mad about this decision, even saying that it was the downfall of America. The families who were plaintiffs in the case received a barrage of hate mail and threats. But a lot of people agreed with SCOTUS's decision and welcomed a prayer-free public school environment. In the years since the *Engel v. Vitale* decision, SCOTUS has ruled over and over again that school-approved religious activity does not have a place in American public schools under the First Amendment.

PRAYER AT A
SCHOOL-SPONSORED EVENT

In 1986, Deborah Weisman and her parents attended her older sister Merith's graduation from Nathan Bishop Middle School in Providence, Rhode Island. It was a normal graduation except for one aspect—at one point, a Baptist minister asked the students and their families to rise and "thank Jesus Christ . . . for making these kids what they are today." The Weismans were Jewish and didn't share the Christian belief that Jesus Christ was a savior. Asking them to thank Jesus was awkward at the least—and sacrilegious at the worst! After hearing the minister's request, Deborah, not sure what to do, looked to her parents for guidance. They were clearly uncomfortable, glancing at all the people standing around them, and reluctantly stood up—and so then, Deborah did too. The Weismans felt humiliated participating in this unexpected religious moment that didn't reflect their own views. After the ceremony, Mr. Weisman complained to the school but didn't receive any reply. He let it go until three years later, when it was fourteen-year-old Deborah's turn to graduate from Nathan Bishop. This time, her dad wanted to make sure their family—and others—didn't suffer the same humiliation from Merith's graduation. He shared his opinion that any kind of religious element to the graduation was inappropriate. In response, he was told by the school: "Don't worry . . . we got you a rabbi."

But that wasn't the point Deborah or her parents were making—they didn't think a public school should require students to take part in *any* kind of prayer. Just because the prayer being offered was one that was more relevant to the Weismans didn't mean it was okay. Their disagreement went unanswered and the rabbi went ahead and stated a prayer at the graduation—one that was carefully crafted at the request of the school to be "nondenominational."

Of course, the Weismans weren't happy and they brought their case to court. By the time Deborah was a junior in high school, her case had reached SCOTUS. The federal appeals court had agreed with her and her family—and SCOTUS did, too, in an opinion named *Lee v. Weisman*. The graduation prayer was an inappropriate state-sponsored and state-directed religious exercise in a public school. It was state-sponsored because the school chose to include a prayer, picked out a clergyperson, provided guidelines, and advised that the prayer should be nonsectarian—so the school even controlled the content of the prayer, forcing everyone to pray in a certain way. In every way, the prayer was directed by the school. Even if they were trying to do things in a way that was respectful to more people.

The school tried to argue that the kids didn't *have* to go to the graduation or they could just choose to ignore the prayer. But graduation is a big deal in kids' lives, SCOTUS pointed out. Even though they technically don't have to be there, it's pretty much obligatory because it's such a major life accomplishment. And kids shouldn't have to choose between attending a ceremony celebrating all their years of hard work or protesting a religious ceremony. As far as ignoring the prayers, SCOTUS thought about what it was really like to be a middle schooler. Kids that age feel more social pressure to do the same thing their peers are doing. If everyone around them was standing up for the prayer, odds are they'd feel like they had to, too. The prayer was not so optional.

While her case was making its way up to the Supreme Court, Deborah spent her high school years known as the kid at the center of this school prayer debacle. Some of her own friends didn't really understand why the graduation prayer was such a big deal to her and her family. But she had an answer: if it's not such a big deal, then it's not a big deal to leave it out. She'd also say kids still had the ability to pray anywhere else—they could even pray in school as long as it wasn't led or endorsed by the school. When SCOTUS handed down its decision that agreed with her, Deborah screamed and hugged her family. They had officially become First Amendment heroes.

SCOTUS has looked at other cases about religion in public schools. These are activities it has ruled inappropriate at public schools:

★ Required daily reading from the Bible

★ Student-led prayer before football games

★ Required posting of the Ten Commandments on the walls of classrooms

★ Voluntary religious education classes during school hours on school property

★ "Moments of silence" for "meditation or voluntary prayer"; however a moment of silence could be okay if "prayer" is not an officially suggested part of it

Students' Right to Practice Religion

So, is any religious activity allowed at school? What if you want to pray on your own? Is that allowed? Can you talk about your religion, someone else's religion, or even mention God? Is public school a completely religion-free zone?

Under the Establishment Clause, all public schools have to avoid school-led or school-sponsored religious activity. But, remember, the Free Exercise Clause allows people to practice their own religion without government interference. So students CAN participate in religion on their own at school. Think of it as two sides of the same coin. Heads is the government speech endorsing religion (not allowed!), and tails is private speech endorsing religion (allowed!).

SCOTUS helped show this distinction in a case called *Westside Community School v. Mergens.* In 1985, high school senior Bridget Mergens wanted to start a Christian Bible study club at her school in Omaha, Nebraska. The school rejected the club—it said it could not provide a teacher sponsor, which was a requirement for new clubs, and the creation of a religious school club would violate the Establishment Clause. The school simply wasn't allowed to have such a club, it said. Bridget took her case to court, and SCOTUS sided with her. SCOTUS okayed student religious clubs on school property as long as participation was voluntary; the club occurred after school hours; it didn't disrupt the school; and a teacher or staff sponsor didn't receive payment for their participation.

As a student, you have the following rights:

- To pray to yourself at any time
- To use a school-sanctioned or approved moment of silence to pray
- To participate in a religious-themed club as long as it takes place after school hours, is voluntary, and is student-led
- To express your religious beliefs at school, in homework, and in school assignments
- To read and study religious materials during recess, lunch, and before or after school
- To pray or discuss religion with other students during the school day, as long as it isn't disruptive and doesn't violate the rights of other students (like their right to learn at school)
- To have your absence excused for religious observances, activities, or holidays

You Be the Judge

· ·

Being open about mental health is important. Kids have stress and anxiety. And, guess what? You need ways to manage them to live a happy life. More than ever before, you'll find students across the country downward-dogging and meditating. Experts say that yoga and meditation have mental health benefits for kids: these practices can help kids better deal with stress and anxiety, focus and learn better, and be kinder and more compassionate.

Both yoga and meditation have roots in religion—yoga in Hinduism and meditation in Buddhism. Many people believe that there's no religious element to the yoga and meditation being done in schools—that it's strictly for mental health purposes. But others are not happy and view these activities as the same as school-led prayer: inappropriate school-sponsored religious activity. Across the country, states have very different opinions.

Alabama passed a law banning yoga in public schools (especially use of the word *namaste*).

But an appeals court in California found that yoga in schools was not a religious activity and therefore didn't violate the First Amendment.

Do you think yoga and meditation should be allowed at schools? Do you think their use in schools is a religious practice?

- To receive an accommodation in school dress codes for clothing or jewelry or hairstyles related to your religious beliefs or practices

- To learn about religion or the Bible from a literary or historic point of view, where the learning doesn't aid or oppose any religion

- To be free from discrimination, bullying, or hate speech because of your religion

LEGAL LINGO

DISCRIMINATION Discrimination is unjust actions toward a person or people, or especially preferential treatment of one person or group over others, because of their race, ethnicity, gender, or sexual orientation.

Monkey Laws and Teaching Evolution in Schools

Sometimes religion has a way of leaking into the things kids learn at school. SCOTUS has had to weigh in twice on religion as it relates to the subject of biology. The theory of human evolution is a scientific theory based on the findings of scientist Charles Darwin that humans originated from apelike ancestors and evolved over millions of years. But for some school districts, evolution doesn't jibe with the Bible's take on the origins of man, the idea that God created all man. Some states went so far as to ban the teaching of evolution in favor of this biblical interpretation in what has been called creation science or intelligent design.

ARKANSAS'S MONKEY LAW

Arkansas was one of those states. It passed a law saying that a teacher at a public school could not "teach theory or doctrine that mankind ascended or descended from a lower order of animals." In other words, no mention of monkey ancestors. Not only was it illegal in Arkansas to teach human evolution—a teacher could actually go to jail for even using a textbook that merely mentioned evolution. You heard that right! Jail, as in, a cell with iron bars and a lifelong criminal conviction just for sharing a book with evolution content inside! But not every Arkansas teacher agreed with this law.

In 1965, Susan Epperson was a twenty-four-year-old Arkansas native and a biology teacher. Although she considered herself a devout Christian, she strongly believed in the theory of evolution. For her classroom, she wanted to use a textbook that had a chapter about evolution and intended to teach the theory to her students. Mrs. Epperson was faced with a choice: (a) Teach her students the biblical story of the origins of humans, something she questioned the scientific truth of, or (b) Teach her students what she believed was science-based fact and face criminal punishment, or even possibly lose her job. Neither option was great. It wasn't fair to have to choose.

Mrs. Epperson decided to bring a case to court challenging Arkansas's "monkey law," as it was jokingly called. The first court said the law was invalid, but the appeals court reversed that decision and said it was constitutional. In 1968, SCOTUS decided to give its opinion on the matter. Mrs. Epperson was the ultimate winner. The ban on teaching evolution science favored one religion's theory over another's, the court said. Arkansas's monkey law was struck down and voided. The rest of the country took note and teachers across the country knew they could teach evolution to their students without fear of punishment.

LOUISIANA CREATIONISM LAW

But the fight for teaching alternative theories on the origin of humans in school was not over. People who really wanted to push for teaching creationism decided to try out a new approach. The biblical theory on the origins of humans was given a fancy new name: "creation science." And instead of banning the teaching of evolution outright, they wondered what would happen if there was a law saying schools had to spend equal time teaching both evolution and creationism. Under this law, not only would religious creation science have to be taught if evolution was taught, but a teacher who disagreed with teaching creation science could only then choose *not* to teach evolution—so the students would learn neither theory. Would SCOTUS allow that law to stand? The state of Louisiana decided to give it a go with its Louisiana creationism law. It wasn't long before the law was challenged in court.

SCOTUS wasn't impressed. In a unanimous decision, it struck down the Louisiana law. Even though the theory was now called creation *science*, it didn't take away the fact that this theory originated in religion and was religious in nature. The Louisiana law clearly had a religious purpose and promoted a Christian belief over others.

Although SCOTUS dismantled the Louisiana creationism law, it did leave room for the teaching of creation science, as well as any other theories on the origins of humankind if they had a nonreligious purpose. In other words, it was okay to teach a theory if it was coming from a purely scientific and academic motivation.

INTELLIGENT DESIGN

The story of teaching evolution in schools is still . . . well, evolving. The latest challenge to teaching evolution and incorporating biblical creation is another alternative theory called "intelligent design." Although it's a slightly different theory from creation science, a federal court found it was just "creationism re-labeled." This argument doesn't seem like a winner either, but SCOTUS has yet to decide on it.

Although human evolutionary science is backed up by nearly two hundred years of scientific research conducted since Charles Darwin first published his findings in *On the Origin of Species* in 1859, many schools still find it controversial and choose to exclude the teaching of human evolution theory from biology class. If they can't teach creation science and the biblical creation of man story, then they choose to teach—nothing. They just skip over that part, leaving students to fill that hole in their education on their own.

Pledge of Allegiance "Under God"

Nearly every kid in America can recite the Pledge of Allegiance by heart. They can practically say it in their sleep. Hand on heart, students say those thirty-one words ending with "one Nation under God, indivisible, with liberty and justice for all," and go on with their school day—no big deal.

But what if it *was* a BIG deal to you?

What if you liked being patriotic, but didn't believe in God or just one god?

What if you were either forced to say the Pledge or felt pressured to because your peers said it without any issue? What if your teachers made you say it? For some, the Pledge can be a daily source of discomfort. A daily moment when they feel like an outsider. Why does the Pledge have to have a mention of God in it anyway?

The Pledge of Allegiance has been around for a long time. An early version was published in a children's magazine in 1892, and was written to honor the four-hundredth anniversary of Christopher Columbus's arrival in America. Within a few decades, it became a regular feature of classroom mornings. But these early versions didn't contain any mention of God. "Under God" didn't insert itself into the Pledge until 1954, when Dwight David Eisenhower was president. Congress passed a law officially including "under God" in the Pledge. This was important to them because of what the country was going through at the time—the Cold War with the Soviet Union (the Soviet Union, before its dissolution, or breakup, in 1991, was made up of the countries that we now call Russia, Ukraine, and thirteen other nations). The Communism the Soviet Union embraced was not seen as something Americans agreed with, and Congress wanted to underline the differences between democracy and Communism in the Pledge. Congress believed that by including "under God" in the Pledge, it distinguished Americans from the officially atheistic Soviet government.

But even before "under God" was included, people had taken issue with the Pledge of Allegiance because of their religion. In 1935, in Minersville, Pennsylvania, Jehovah's Witness siblings, twelve-year-old Lillian Gobitis and ten-year-old William Gobitis, refused to say the Pledge at school and were expelled. Jehovah's Witnesses are members of a religion that believes God's Kingdom is their government, and to recite the Pledge is a form of inappropriate worship of another government. In other words, it was against their religion to say the Pledge. In 1940, SCOTUS ruled on a lawsuit brought by Lillian and William's angry parents called *Minersville School District v. Gobitis*. Shockingly, SCOTUS sided with the school and ruled that it had the right to expel the siblings for refusing to say the Pledge. The Pledge wasn't religious, the justices said.

After SCOTUS's *Gobitis* decision, Jehovah's Witnesses across the country became targets of bigotry and prejudice. Haters must have felt like the justices had okayed this behavior: "They're traitors; the Supreme Court says so. Ain't you heard?" said one sheriff. There were incidents of Jehovah's Witness worship spaces being burned down, religious members being beaten and even tarred and feathered. Over two thousand Jehovah's Witness students were expelled from school. Many children were whipped as punishment for not saying the Pledge.

Just three years later, SCOTUS did a complete one-eighty—the justices realized they had made a huge mistake in deciding the way they did in the *Gobitis* case. In a new case called *West Virginia State Board of Education v. Barnette*, a pair of elementary-school-aged Jehovah's Witness sisters named Marie and Gathie were instructed by their parents not to say the Pledge.

They bravely complied, refused to say the Pledge, and were then expelled from their school. Every day, they tried to return to school, but were turned away. This time, SCOTUS ruled opposite of what it did in the *Gobitis* case: the school was violating Marie's and Gathie's First Amendment rights by punishing them for not saying the Pledge. This was a huge win for Jehovah's Witnesses and helped put an end to the many hate-fueled attacks.

Issues surrounding the Pledge of Allegiance and the First Amendment seemed settled—that is, until the words "under God" were added. Over the years and across many states, students have fought with public schools over whether being required to recite the Pledge of Allegiance violates their religious freedom rights because of the inclusion of "under God." There were instances of kids being forced to stand outside in the rain for refusing to say the Pledge, getting detention, being ridiculed or kicked out of class, being called unpatriotic.

In all of these cases, courts have upheld the right to include "under God" in the Pledge. For the most part, judges have focused on the fact that even

though the Pledge mentions God, the Pledge itself isn't really religious. It was written for patriotic purposes—not for religious purposes. There are mentions of God in other places in American government, like the national motto "In God We Trust"—we wouldn't change the motto and take it off our currency, would we? Here's where things stand today: a school can't require a student to say the Pledge, but the Pledge can remain a fixture in public schools.

In 2004, one "under God" Pledge case did make it all the way up to the Supreme Court, a case called *Elk Grove Unified School District v. Newdow*. On behalf of his nine-year-old daughter, atheist Michael Newdow challenged the Pledge, saying its reference to God made it unconstitutional under the First Amendment. SCOTUS agreed to review his case—but not the central "under God" question. Mr. Newdow lost his case for a procedural reason: he didn't have legal custody of his daughter, so he didn't have the right to bring the case in the first place, SCOTUS decided. Even though the justices didn't get to ultimately decide the big Pledge question, some of the justices didn't want to miss the opportunity to give a preview of how they *would* rule if given the chance to decide the "under God" issue. In three concurring opinions, three justices signed on to the belief that the Pledge did NOT violate the First Amendment. It reflected America's religious history, but was not a religious activity.

For now, the Pledge of Allegiance in its current form seems like it's here to stay.

LEGAL LINGO

CONCURRING OPINION When a justice agrees on the main holding of the case but has different reasons for agreeing, they write their own opinion explaining why, which is called a concurring opinion.

The Pledge of Allegiance isn't the only place in American government and history that references God. Other important mentions include the following:

★ Declaration of Independence (four mentions)

★ US Constitution (Article VII includes "the Year of our Lord")

★ All fifty state constitutions (God or a divine being is mentioned at least once)

★ The national motto, which appears on US currency ("In God We Trust")

★ The Presidential Oath stated during inauguration ("So help me God")

★ Abraham Lincoln's Gettysburg Address (contained fourteen references to God in its 699 words)

Religious Clothing at School

In 2003, twelve-year-old sixth grader Nashala Hearn started at Benjamin Franklin Science Academy, a public school in Muskogee, Oklahoma. It had been a couple of weeks, and so far, everything was going fine. No one had made a fuss about her hijab, which she, a practicing Muslim, wore because she believed dressing modestly and covering her hair with a headscarf were ways to honor Allah. Her mom had even informed her homeroom teacher, Mrs. Walker, about it, and Mrs. Walker had understood. But then came the two-year anniversary of the September 11 terrorist attacks on the World Trade Center. Mrs. Walker told Nashala that she shouldn't wear her hijab because it could potentially frighten other students. She sent Nashala to the principal's office. The principal informed Nashala that she was no longer allowed to wear her hijab because it violated the "no hats" policy at school. She had to take it off. Nashala didn't understand—a hijab was a headscarf, not a hat. And she couldn't take it off without going against her religious beliefs. She told the principal she absolutely couldn't remove it. For this, she received a three-day suspension and was told to return to school bareheaded.

Nashala had been wearing her hijab for weeks and no one had told her it was against the rules. And even if her hijab was considered a hat, there were lots of exceptions to the "no hat" rule at school—like special "hat days" in support of programs or celebrations and with costumes for Halloween and plays. Surely, the school could grant an exception for her if her religion required her to wear this head covering? The only thing that made sense to the Hearns was that the school's actions were part of the racist anti-Muslim sentiment that had developed after the September 11 attacks. Nashala had thought her new school was a safe space from that, but now she wasn't so sure.

When Nashala returned to school wearing her hijab, she was issued a second suspension. Her family knew that Nashala had a right to wear religious clothing at school under the First Amendment and filed a lawsuit against the school district. The federal court agreed the school district was wrong and had violated Nashala's constitutional rights. The court ordered the school district to let her wear her hijab to school and required that any student with religious beliefs that conflicted with school policies be allowed an accommodation. Stated in another way: schools had to respect the religious beliefs of students. Students should never be put in the position where they have to choose between abiding by their religion and getting their public school education.

Courts and lawmakers have required schools across the country to make accommodations for students who wish to wear religious clothing. Accommodations should be made for the following types of clothing:

★ Hijabs and other forms of head coverings worn by Muslim females

★ Kufis, skullcaps worn by Muslim males

★ Yarmulkes, skullcaps worn by Jewish males

★ Turbans worn by both Sikh men and women

★ Red hair band in honor of Native American heritage

★ Crucifix necklace worn by Christians

★ Star of David necklace worn by Jews

★ Rosary beads carried or worn by Catholics

★ Any other piece of clothing or jewelry that is worn in accordance with religion

·················· **GLOBAL PERSPECTIVE** ··················

FRANCE

France has the same goal as the United States: religious tolerance. But it goes about it in a very different way. Instead of making accommodations at public schools for every religion, France makes *no* accommodations for *any* religion. In France, a student cannot attend public school wearing any kind of religious garb or symbol. For kids who must wear religious clothing or jewelry, they have to be homeschooled or attend private school. In 2021, France's Senate voted to ban anyone under the age of eighteen from wearing religious garments in public—so, in addition to school, girls wouldn't be able to wear their hijabs in public streets, parks, or buildings. Cleverly, these laws do not mention any particular religious symbol. So equal bans exist for Christian crosses, Sikh turbans, Jewish yarmulkes, Muslim hijabs, and all other religious symbols. Regardless, many French believe these laws target Muslim schoolgirls' khimar headscarves, which is an essential article of faith as part of the hijab—a garment that covers the hair, neck, and all or part of the chest, but not the face. The vote caused fury across the world, especially in France, sparking protest, including a #HandsOffMy-Hijab social media campaign. There will surely be more to come on this issue in France.

MEDIA
PRESS
VOICE
PETITION
RALLY
JUSTIC
EXPRESSION
MARCH
PROTEST
FREEDOM
ASSOCIATION
RELIGION
ASSEMBLY
SPEECH
RIGHTS

4 ⟩ Freedom of Speech

Now it's time to talk about the most famous of all First Amendment rights—freedom of speech. Also known as freedom of expression, freedom of speech is one of the fundamental rights that Americans are most proud of and hold most dear. We love to talk about our freedom of speech. We love to remind others that we have the right to express ourselves freely.

Under the Constitution, the US government is not allowed to make laws that interfere with its citizens' speech or what people talk about. With some limits, our government can't stop citizens from saying whatever they want, about whomever they want. The government can't even stop you from talking about the government itself, even if what you're saying is super harsh or mean. Things like: "I don't trust my government" or "I hate my government" or "I want my government to change this policy."

Right about now, you might be thinking of ways to use these power-packed newly discovered rights. How to start? Do you start simply with protesting the painfully limited menu in the cafeteria, which still does not offer you gluten-free pizza? Or do you insist that your principal allow you to make a speech during gym class about any brilliant to mediocre idea that comes to your brain? Hold on to that mic. There *are* limits to free speech, and it is equally important to know those legal limits.

Think about it. There have to be exceptions in order to protect people from really bad effects of certain kinds of speech. For example, the government has the right to punish speech that may cause violence or lots of harm—like if someone yells "Fire!" in a packed theater while knowing for sure there's no fire. A theater-full of people trying to escape an imaginary fire could cause a lot of injuries and panic. That speech can't be protected by the First Amendment because of the near-certain wreckage it creates.

Over the years, SCOTUS has figured out that there are exceptions to freedom of speech, which means there are times when speech can be limited and/or punished. The government can make laws banning these kinds of speech or punish someone who makes them. These are the kinds of speech SCOTUS has ruled are unprotected by the First Amendment:

- Speech that is likely to incite violence or criminal activity
- Speech known as "fighting words," or speech that is a true threat of violence toward others
- Speech that is untrue but said purposefully to harm someone and that person is actually harmed by the false words (This kind of speech is known as *libel* when it's written down and *slander* when it's spoken out loud.)
- Obscene and vulgar speech
- Pornographic photos, videos, or audio featuring underage children
- Speech owned by other people (Copyright protects people's creative works so that other people can't steal or plagiarize them.)
- Threats to the president's life or threats to kidnap or bodily harm him or her

○ False or misleading advertising (Commercial speech or speech in advertisements enjoy less protection than regular speech so that consumers aren't tricked into buying products.)

Also, sometimes the government is allowed to limit *how* and *when* someone expresses themselves, but only with really important and valid reasons to make those limits. For example, a town is allowed to require a group to get a permit to hold a protest rally because disrupting traffic and keeping the streets safe for protesters and nonprotesters alike are important justifications. And that gym class speech? Your principal has good reason to say that's not a good time for you to give it because it will disrupt your classmates' right to exercise and learn. Save that speech for lunchtime.

For the most part, Americans can speak freely and live unafraid of being punished by the government for giving their opinions, no matter how unpopular those opinions are. What's great about this is that it allows for lots of different points of view. Even though sometimes it's painful or infuriating to hear someone's position that you completely disagree with, there's actually something beautiful about the fact that you both have the equal right to be heard. In other countries, you can be jailed—or worse—for speaking up against the government or saying something controversial. In America, we have the great privilege of being able to speak our minds. And it's not just what comes out of your mouth that's protected. Free speech under the First Amendment also applies to the clothes you wear, the music you make, and the poems you write. It protects any form of self-expression from government interference.

This right to speak your mind is for all Americans—**even kids!** But remember the First Amendment applies to the government and not to parents—your parents can still prevent you from telling the world your sister has rotten teeth or that you think BTS is the best boy band in history ever or that you don't like your principal. But the First Amendment does protect you against being punished by the government for expressing yourself. And here's a key detail that you should remember: this protection covers PUBLIC SCHOOLS. So, if your school is funded by the government, the protection applies!

LEGAL LINGO

AMERICAN CIVIL LIBERTIES UNION The American Civil Liberties Union, known as the ACLU, is one of the country's fiercest defenders of the First Amendment. It was originally founded in 1920 as a nonprofit organization "to defend and preserve the individual rights and liberties guaranteed to every person in this country by the Constitution of the United States of America." ACLU lawyers represent people across the country who believe their First Amendment rights have been violated. Some of the most important cases in First Amendment history were legal battles fought by the ACLU, including many of the cases we talk about in this book. The ACLU has represented all kinds of plaintiffs in First Amendment cases, including unpopular ones, like the members of an Illinois Nazi party. Lawyers who work at the ACLU know that sometimes they'll have to represent plaintiffs they think are horrible people who said horrible things—and they do all of this because they believe so strongly in defending Americans' First Amendment right to freedom of speech.

Hate Speech

Plain and simple, in America, hate speech is protected under the First Amendment. Hate speech is mean, horrible, offensive speech expressing hate toward a person or group based on their race, skin color, religion, nation of origin, ethnicity, disability, gender, or sexual orientation. America is pretty unique in this. Many countries criminalize hate speech, meaning people can be fined or can go to jail for using hate speech. But in America the Nazi Party or the Ku Klux Klan has as much of a right to parade in the streets as LGBTQ+ Pride celebrants, Moms Against Drunk Driving, and the Boy Scouts. SCOTUS has even upheld the speech rights of a hate group, the Westboro Baptist Church, which regularly pickets military funerals of American soldiers killed in Iraq, holding up signs that say: "Thank God for Dead Soldiers," "You're Going to Hell," and "God Hates You." Why would Americans want to allow this kind of awful speech?

The theory is this: With the good, comes the bad. If we are really and truly committed to granting free speech to everyone, we need to be okay with allowing every viewpoint: the opinions we love, the opinions we are indifferent to . . . AND the opinions we loathe. It's all part of the deal.

However, that doesn't mean people are allowed to make hateful threats toward others. If hate speech overlaps with one of the unprotected forms of speech—like, if it incites violence—then it can be punished or limited. Otherwise, in America, speech expressing love and hate, speech expressing terrific beliefs or thoughts and truly terrible ideas, and speech expressing popular and unpopular ideas are equally protected.

Symbolic Speech

Speech doesn't always mean spoken or written words. Some-times, an action or a symbol can be a form of expression even when no actual words are involved. Symbolic speech is protected by the First Amendment, too. Some examples of symbolic speech include the following:

o Wearing a T-shirt with the logo of your favorite sports team

o Doing a celebration dance after a teacher announces no homework over the weekend

o Carrying a vegan leather purse instead of an animal leather purse because of your support for animal rights

o Pinning a Black Lives Matter pin to your shirt

o Piercing nine holes in your ears because you like the way it looks

o Giving your parents the silent treatment after they've punished you

Freedom of Speech the Right vs. Freedom of Speech the Culture

In January 2021, President Donald Trump was kicked off social media platforms like Twitter, Facebook, and YouTube after his supporters stormed the US Capitol Building to protest his election loss to Joseph R. Biden, an incident that resulted in the evacuation of Congress and the deaths of five people. Many, including these social media companies, believed that comments President Trump made had incited the incident. They felt it was too dangerous to allow him to continue posting on these platforms. You may be wondering how these social media companies were allowed to shut down the president of the United States. Wouldn't that violate free speech?

Remember, the First Amendment only protects people from the *government's* action—it doesn't protect people from nongovernmental parties, like private companies or individual people. Social media companies have the right to suspend or boot anyone who doesn't abide by their rules, and that includes government officials like the president. More so, these corporations, which include social media powerhouses, have the right to change or alter their rules and regulations. So what's allowed one year can be on the get-booted-off list the very next.

Many Americans were upset President Trump was silenced in this way. They saw him as a victim of "cancel culture"—he was being shunned or censored—and many felt like the bans were against the spirit of free speech (even though they weren't illegal). Letting people speak their mind is a part of American culture. And thus, many believe that silencing someone, especially a president, goes against that.

GLOBAL PERSPECTIVE

THAILAND

In Thailand, it's illegal to insult or criticize any member of the royal family. It can get you sent to prison for a really long time! This anticriticism law is even applied to kids. In May 2021, seventeen-year-old Thanakorn Phiraban was charged with insulting the monarchy *lese majeste*, which means after he spoke at a pro-democracy rally. He faces between three to fifteen years in prison.

Speech at School

MARY BETH TINKER AND STUDENTS' RIGHT TO SPEAK UP

Have you ever gotten so mad at a policy or action made by your school that you wanted to protest against it? Have you ever been so upset by something unjust that's happened in your school or in the news that you want to show your support for a cause or as an ally? Would you even be allowed to speak up? Or organize a protest or a walkout?

We know how to answer these last two questions—all because of an eighth-grade girl named Mary Beth Tinker. In 1965, the Vietnam War was raging overseas. Back home, America's involvement in the war was really unpopular, especially with young people. After seeing images of body bags and displaced children on the news, Mary Beth was sad and angry and felt a deep need to show her opposition to the war. Her older brother, John, a high school student, agreed with her and helped figure out a way they could show their antiwar sentiment at school—they, along with John's friend Christopher Eckhardt, decided to wear black armbands emblazoned with peace signs.

Mary Beth, the only one in middle school, bravely walked into Warren Harding Junior High alone, her black armband in view to everyone. She didn't even take it off when her friends warned she was going to get into trouble. School district officials did not like this act of opposition, and they definitely didn't want other students to join in. They quickly passed a rule saying students couldn't wear armbands. Mary Beth, John, and Chris wore them again anyway and were all suspended.

The students then filed a court case, saying that, by suspending them, the school district had violated their rights to free speech under the First Amendment. The case went all the way up to SCOTUS—and they won! The SCOTUS justices reviewed both the school district's interest in maintaining a place of learning for all students and the students' rights to free speech, weighing them against each other. The judges decided that the armbands weren't particularly disruptive to learning and that Mary Beth had the right to protest in this particular way.

This was a HUGE victory for students—the biggest free speech victory for kids EVER. For the first time, the highest court in the country was

saying that kids have free speech rights in school. In his opinion on the case, a justice famously said that students don't "shed their constitutional rights to freedom of speech or expression at the schoolhouse gate." In other words, public school teachers and administrators don't have the right to silence kids.

Thanks to Mary Beth Tinker, we know that students DO have the right to protest at school. Great! So can you go ahead and stage a walkout and not face punishment? Well, that's a murkier point. A student protest can't be overly disruptive of learning, which means it has to be peaceful and it can't be lewd, vulgar, or violent. A school does have the right to ban or punish protests that get in the way of other kids' right to learn. What's considered overly disruptive? Every school and student will have a different opinion on this. That's one reason why First Amendment cases filed by students are still being reviewed by courts today.

If a protest occurs during school hours and students miss class, a school can discipline them for missing school—just like it would if students missed class for any other unexcused reason. What a school *can't* do is punish a student *more* because they skipped for a protest specifically. In other words, students can't be punished extra because they were expressing their opinion, even when it's opposed to the school's belief. If you're planning a midday protest, a good first step is to check your school's policies (usually located in a student handbook) on unexcused absences and truancy.

Guide to Planning a School Protest

Civil protests are an American tradition! Here are some pointers on how to successfully protest:

1. **WORK ON PROTESTS THAT INSPIRE YOU.** Choose a cause or stand up for something you really believe in.

2. **SEEK ALLIES.** Numbers matter. If you feel passionate about an important cause, chances are, so does someone else you know.

3. **CHECK YOUR SCHOOL'S POLICIES.** Know what the punishments are for unexcused absences if you are planning on missing more than a few days of class. Look closely at what triggers suspension and your rights to make up missed work.

4. **TAKE IT OFF CAMPUS.** This makes it harder for schools to say the protest is disruptive.

5. **SCHEDULE IT OUTSIDE OF SCHOOL OR LEARNING HOURS.** This also makes it harder for schools to say the protest is disruptive and eliminates the chance of discipline for missing class.

6. **CONSIDER WEARING YOUR PROTEST.** Wearing a piece of clothing that expresses your opinion is likely less disruptive than staging a walkout.

7. **DON'T USE VULGAR OR OFFENSIVE LANGUAGE.** Just don't. It will make your protest stronger if you don't resort to this.

8. **DON'T INCITE VIOLENCE.** Ever. If a student protest makes an unsafe environment for kids, that overrules any free speech rights.

KID FIRST AMENDMENT HERO: AN INTERVIEW WITH

MARY BETH TINKER

Mary Beth Tinker is still a First Amendment activist today,
speaking all over the country about the importance of
freedom of speech—especially for kids!

What inspired you to wear a black armband of protest?

In 1963, I witnessed the Birmingham Children's Crusade during which almost two thousand kids and teens were arrested that year in Alabama. These kids were really the Black Lives Matter from that era. Then there was the 16th Street Baptist Church bombing that killed four little girls. I admired civil rights activist Bayard Rustin, who had put out a letter to wear black armbands to mourn for the little girls. That was my first experience with black armbands. I was really inspired by the kids who came before me.

Did anyone else inspire you?

My mother was also involved in an organization called CORE—the Congress of Racial Equality. My dad was a Methodist minister. My parents raised us to believe in justice and love and understanding, all the things you get from your faith.

What did your parents say when they learned of your plan to protest the Vietnam War this way?

My dad said: "I don't think y'all should wear those black armbands because the principal has made a rule against it. You know it's not so easy to be a principal." He pretty much believed in rules. He was conservative that way. My brother John said, "Dad, you know this is a piece of black cloth and people are dying. We're just wanting to wear this little piece of black cloth." My dad had always taught us to "speak up for our conscience." So, when we told him "Dad, this is our conscience," he supported us.

You were the only middle school protester. Were there moments when you felt alone?

> I felt alone quite a bit in many ways growing up. I really was just a shy girl, a regular kid. I had some friends at school. On the day of the protest, my friend Connie thought I should take off the armband. And I was supposed to get this petition signed, too. That was the plan, for the students to sign a petition. Well, I got only one signature on there! And even though I took my armband off when the principal asked me to, I was still able to make an impact.

What did it feel like to be a First Amendment hero in the news, especially being a shy girl?

> It was crazy. I had to go for depositions and when I went to the appeals court hearing in St. Louis, that was first time I flew on an airplane. I was fifteen. I remember walking to the courthouse across the street, I noticed that my stockings weren't right. You know, I was worried about that. How to dress right. It was very intimidating. It was even crazier after we won. We had moved and I was at a new school. I was still quiet and shy, barely had any friends, and helicopters from *Time* magazine were flying in to interview me. It was a lot.

After the case blew up into national news, were there any safety issues?

> People did threaten us. By this time, we did know there were crazy dangerous people out there. A woman called on the phone threatening to kill me. People threw red paint at our house, a brick at our car window, and sent hate mail.

Were there any moments you regretted speaking up?

> No, I have to say, I never really felt that. I just felt like: this isn't fair. We were just wearing this little piece of cloth on our arms. It wasn't hurting anybody. Kids have a great sense of fairness. When they see something unfair, they feel it strongly. And adults tell kids "Oh, life's not fair. Get used to it." I like to tell the kids: "Life should be fair."

You Be the Judge

In 2018, in response to recent school shooting tragedies, high school students across the country coordinated walkouts and "die ins," where students demonstrated their support for more gun control and school safety measures. Having gotten wind of students' plans, one Texas school district took to social media to warn students that they would face consequences, including suspension, for any actions taken during the school day.

Do you think this is a violation of students' free speech and their right to protest? Why or why not? If you were the judge on this case, what would you do?

I CAN WEAR WHATEVER I WANT—CAN'T I?

Clothing is just about what you wear, right? Far from it! It isn't just for keeping your body warm in the winter or looking trendy at your friend's birthday party. Clothing triggers many potential legal issues—especially since it's a form of self-expression. **EXPRESSION = FIRST AMENDMENT.** By choosing to wear a particular item of clothing, you're sending a message to those who see you. For example, if you wear a band T-shirt, you're saying: "I think this band is cool." If you wear a T-shirt from a political candidate's campaign, you're saying: "I think this politician should get elected." If you wear a hijab, you're saying: "I'm proud of my religion and culture." And if you wear clothes that are gender-nonconforming, you're saying: "This is me." Just like other forms of expression, the clothes you wear to school are protected by the First Amendment.

Mary Beth Tinker's case was about a piece of clothing—an armband. In her case, and many others, student clothing is used as a form of protest. When it comes to kids' expression at school, a court asks: Is it overly disruptive to learning and other students' rights? In other words, are you wearing something that totally throws kids off their main focus, which is school? Whether a piece of clothing is disruptive or not depends on all sorts of circumstances, and the answer may be different for different schools. If a school does ban a student from wearing certain types of clothing, it has to be able to justify that ban by showing the clothing is taking other students' focus away from their education.

This brings us to something you're probably familiar with. Many schools have dress codes that prohibit certain types of clothing, such as short skirts or sweatpants or T-shirts with slogans on them. In general, dress codes are allowed as long as the bans are "content-neutral," which means the school doesn't favor one kind of expression over another. For example, a school can't ban clothing supporting the New York Yankees, but allow clothing supporting the New York Mets.

Most importantly, a school can't ban an article of clothing just because it goes against the school's beliefs. Freedom of speech has helped to protect girls, children of color, disabled students, and LGBTQ+ students from clothing bans by schools who disfavor them.

Across the country, students have pushed back against schools' bans on their clothing under First Amendment grounds.

Here are some examples of student clothing that courts have held are protected by freedom of speech:

o Black armbands as antiwar protest

o Rosaries, headscarves, and other religious symbols

o A T-shirt with a picture of President George W. Bush and the words "International Terrorist"

o A T-shirt supporting the National Rifle Association featuring an image of guns

o A band T-shirt with "666" on it

o Breast cancer awareness bracelets that read "I ♥ Boobies"

o Rainbow belts and writing "Gay Pride" or "GP" on skin or clothing in support of LGBTQ+ rights

Here are some examples where courts have upheld (allowed) school bans on student clothing:

o Clothing worn to show gang association

o Clothing promoting illegal drug use

o Clothing bearing Confederate flags

o A T-shirt that said "Drugs suck"

o Student shirts with opposing views on immigration, one set saying "Border Patrol," and the other set, "We Are Not Criminals"

In two different court cases, schools suspended kids for wearing clothing they thought was lewd or vulgar. One decision was in favor of students, one was in favor of the school. Do you think these cases were rightly decided?

I ♥ BOOBIES

In 2010, seventh graders Kayla Martinez and Brianna Hawk wore rubber bracelets promoting breast cancer awareness that read "I ♥ Boobies (Keep a Breast)" to school. They did this even though their Easton, Pennsylvania, middle school issued a ban on the bracelets and other "boobie" gear after it became popular with students. With the permission of their parents, Kayla and Brianna ignored the ban and were suspended.

The girls knew this was unfair and took their case to court. The school argued that the bracelets were lewd and vulgar and distracted other students, but a federal court sided with Kayla and Brianna, saying this form of speech was intended to be an act of solidarity with family members affected by breast cancer and to raise awareness among their peers. The court also found there were a lot of different dictionary definitions of the word "boobies" and the word wasn't vulgar on its own. There was no issue with "♥" either. When you "♥" something, it doesn't necessarily mean anything sexual. Also, the school didn't show that it thought the word "boobies" was so vulgar when it used the word during the announcement of the ban to the entire school. There were no major incidents of disruption. The girls and any Easton students should have been free to wear their bracelets.

DRUGS SUCK!

In 1992, Norfolk, Virginia, seventh grader and boy band fan Kimberly Broussard wore to school a "Drugs Suck!" T-shirt that she bought at a New Kids on the Block concert.

Almost immediately, Kimberly was asked to turn her shirt inside out or wear another shirt because the school felt the word "suck" was vulgar and offensive. Kimberly refused and was given a one-day suspension. She brought her case to court, saying her First Amendment rights were violated. The whole case was arguing over the word "suck"!

At thirteen years old, Kimberly testified in federal court, saying she wanted to get the word out that "it's not right to use drugs." She didn't think of the word "suck" as having sexual meaning but that it just meant that you thought something was bad. Even though the court called her "mature and articulate," it disagreed with her. It said most middle schoolers know it's a word with sexual connotations. Even when being used to show disapproval, the word was still based on a vulgar meaning. Because the word was vulgar to her middle school classmates, it was likely to cause a disruption and the school had a right to regulate student language in this way and promote "socially appropriate speech."

Your Hair, Your Crown

Hair is part of your ultimate physical identity. From buzz cuts to mohawks, box braids to twists, hair means a lot of different things to different people. To some, it's the unruly bane of their existence or just the fuzzy thing that sits on top of their head. To others, it's a source of pride, a representation of culture or religion, or carefully crafted proof of your coolness. C'mon, people! It's not *just* hair, right?

Are hairstyles seen as a kind of symbolic speech, like clothes are? The answer to that is not entirely clear. SCOTUS has not taken up a case on this exact issue just yet, so we don't know for sure what the law of the land is. That means there is no set rule for the entire country to follow. But many people and many courts have spoken out already, and so far, many seem to think that hairstyles DO present a freedom of speech issue.

Just like with clothes, some schools have tried to impose rules about what hairstyles kids are (or aren't) allowed to wear. Sometimes, those rules target kids from certain cultures or races over others. Like, if a school bans dreadlocks, that's probably going to affect Black students more than white students because dreadlocks are associated more with Black culture. So isn't the school banning Black culture by banning dreadlocks? Many people—including lawmakers—think so.

In 2018, sixteen-year-old Andrew Johnson's face flashed across the national news. It was not for his scholastic achievements or skillful athletic moves on the wrestling mat. No, it was for his hair. His beloved dreadlocked hair that was sliced off at a school wrestling match. On that day, Andrew learned firsthand what it felt like to be subject to a racially motivated hair ban.

Andrew, who is mixed race, was set to start his high school wrestling match in Buena Vista, New Jersey. But there was a problem. It didn't have to do with his training or his uniform or his team—it had to do with his hair. Andrew wore dreadlocks and the referee took issue with that. The rules stated wrestlers' hair had to be in a "natural state."

"Dreadlocks aren't natural," the referee told Andrew and his coach. He gave Andrew ninety seconds to decide—either cut off your hair or forfeit the match.

Andrew loved his locs but wanted to compete. Everyone, including his mom and grandpa, watched what was happening from the stands. The clock was ticking. Andrew didn't want to let his team down, so he decided to cut them. His team's trainer snipped them off while an emotional Andrew held back tears. The crowd booed—they didn't think this was right. Andrew went on to win his match, but after it was over, he ran out of the gym in tears, humiliated.

The incident was picked up by the national media and many were outraged, believing the referee unfairly targeted Andrew because of his race. Many believed New Jersey's school wrestling rule that competitors' hair had to be in a "natural state" targeted students who were Black. It wasn't fair. In the end, officials removed "natural state" from the rules and the referee was banned for two years. Andrew went on to compete as a high school wrestler.

Shocked yet? Well, hold on because Andrew's story isn't the only one of its kind. Although his has been one of the more public stories, and ignited a call for change, here are a few more incidents that occurred within one year of Andrew's story: A female high school student with Native American heritage in New Mexico had a portion of her long braids cut off by her teacher. An eleven-year-old New Jersey girl was kicked out of her middle school for wearing braided hair extensions. A six-year-old in Florida was sent home on the first day at his new school for wearing dreadlocks. A set of twin high school girls in Massachusetts were given detention for wearing their hair in braids. School administrators filled in a Texas middle schooler's fade with a black Sharpie marker.

All of this unfairness helped motivate the passing of the CROWN Act in many states, starting in 2019. CROWN stands for Create a Respectful and Open Workplace for Natural Hair. This act helps prevent discrimination against race-based hairstyles both for kids at school and adults at work. This protects kids from facing school discipline over natural textured hairstyles or protective hairstyles like braids, locs, twists, and knots. California was the first to adopt the CROWN Act. Andrew Johnson's state of New Jersey soon followed, as well as many other states. Also in 2019, Cory Booker, a senator from New Jersey, proposed to make a version of the CROWN Act a federal law.

You Be the Judge

What if you want to dye your hair green? Or wear your hair in a non-gender-conforming way? As we've mentioned, some courts have said that a hairstyle *is* a form of expression called symbolic speech and should be protected by the First Amendment. Other courts say that hairstyles are not the same as verbal or written speech or even expression through clothing. These courts ruled that schools have a right to ban certain hairstyles because of their interest in eliminating classroom distraction and avoiding tension between students.

    If you were a SCOTUS justice, how would you decide? Why is a hairstyle like speech or why isn't it? Do you think the school's reasons for banning certain hairstyles are important enough to outweigh students' freedom of speech?

Speech That Takes Place Away from School

Fourteen-year-old Pennsylvania freshman Brandi Levy was in a sour mood. Can you blame her? She had just found out that she hadn't made the varsity cheerleading team. What really bugged her was that she'd been told freshman girls needed a year on the JV squad before they could make varsity—but she knew of an incoming freshman girl who had scored a spot.

And the bad news just kept coming. She hadn't gotten the right fielder position she wanted on her private softball team, either. School finals were approaching and everything felt unfair. She needed to vent, so she did what lots of kids do when they're frustrated: she whipped out her cell phone.

On a Saturday in 2017, Brandi was standing outside of a convenience store with a friend. She opened her Snapchat app and took a selfie giving the middle finger to the camera. Brandi added a caption to the photo: "F*** school f*** softball f*** cheer f*** everything," and posted it. She added, in another post, "Love how me and [her friend] get told we need a year of jv before we make varsity but that's [*sic*] doesn't matter to anyone else? 😫"

"I wasn't really thinking about how this would turn out," Brandi said later. "Or, like, how people would react to it."

This F-bomb-laden Snap doesn't sound like the makings of a major Supreme Court battle, but it was.

Even though Snapchats disappear after twenty-four hours, Brandi had about 250 friends who could have seen it, including members of her cheer squad. At least one of them screenshotted Brandi's Snap and shared it with other teammates. Eventually, that soon-to-be famous Snap made its way to a teammate who happened to be the daughter of a coach. Unhappy about Brandi's take on her team, the coach's daughter showed the photo to her mom. Other teammates complained about Brandi's posts to their coaches.

Things continued to quickly go downhill from there. For the upcoming year, Brandi got suspended from her team for violating the team's rules, which required that students "have respect" for the school, coaches, and teammates; avoid "foul language and inappropriate gestures"; and refrain from sharing "negative information regarding cheerleading, cheerleaders or coaches . . . on the internet." Her coaches, along with school administrators, also claimed that she violated a school rule that student athletes must conduct themselves during the season "in such a way that the image of the Mahanoy School District would not be tarnished in any manner."

This suspension didn't sit well with Brandi. "That's just how fourteen-year-old teenagers talk, how everyone talked," she thought. And it didn't seem fair that she should get kicked off a school team for speech she made on a Saturday, when she wasn't even at school. Was the school stomping all over her First Amendment rights? Teaming up with the ACLU, Brandi filed a lawsuit against her school in a case that became famous as *Mahanoy Area School District v. B.L.* At the heart of it was an important legal question that had been confusing schools and courts across the country for years: Can public schools punish students for speech they make off campus?

This question forces us to confront a lot of other really tough questions. Let's break it down!

First—if you recall—under the *Tinker* case decision, student speech can be limited only if it substantially disrupts school. But can something that happens *off campus* actually make a substantial disruption *on campus*?

Second—now that practically every kid has a cell phone glued to their hands, which usually also allows for access to social media, where is the line drawn? That means, what counts as *on-campus* speech and *off-campus* speech? Couldn't something that happens on social media be disruptive to school whether it was posted at school or somewhere else? What about bullying on social media? Couldn't a school punish a kid for bullying? And during the pandemic, home-based learning became the norm; what's considered off campus, if your "campus" is now your home?

Third—what if schools can regulate off-campus speech? Does that mean schools can limit student speech 24/7? Shouldn't parents be able to parent their kids without interference from the school?

This case wasn't just about the varsity cheerleading team and how offended people were at a few F-bombs launched by a ticked-off Pennsylvania teen on a Saturday shopping spree at her local convenience store. Brandi's case was a legal minefield swarming with essential free speech questions that American schools nationwide had been eagerly awaiting clear answers. When Brandi's case got accepted for review by SCOTUS in 2021, every public school in the country was paying attention.

Brandi's legal position was clear: her speech was made off campus, over the weekend, and on her own cell phone. Therefore, she believed, the school did not have the right to punish her for this kind of speech. It had violated the First Amendment when it suspended her from a school team because of her social media post.

The school had a different take: Whether she made the social media post at school or somewhere else, the impact of the post was the same. Her post upset her teammates and caused a substantial disruption. The school, it believed, had the right to punish Brandi for her speech.

In one of the biggest student speech victories in decades, SCOTUS sided with Brandi by a landslide. Eight of the nine SCOTUS justices agreed that the school violated Brandi's First Amendment rights in this particular case, under these particular facts. Importantly, SCOTUS left a window open for future cases on *off-campus* student speech. Specifically, SCOTUS said there probably *are* cases when a school can regulate *off-campus* speech—but this wasn't one of them.

SCOTUS believed that in most situations, schools shouldn't regulate *off-campus* speech because of **three** reasons:

o First, a student's off-campus speech should be the responsibility of their parents. Parents have the right to punish their kids for the things they say.

o Second, if a school has the right to regulate off-campus speech all the time, that means it could regulate basically everything a student says or does outside of school—and that's just not fair.

o Third, schools *should* be protecting unpopular opinions and ideas by its students. That's what the First Amendment is all about!

If we're being honest with ourselves, Brandi's Snap certainly wasn't the most eloquent or respectful bit of writing. But, whittled down to its core, Brandi's speech was essentially a criticism of the school, a community she was a member of. It's important for community members to be allowed to criticize communities they are a part of. Her post didn't even identify the school by name or target any specific people. When she made the post, she believed it would be seen only by her private circle of Snapchat friends. It didn't cause any substantial disruption at school. Even though some of her teammates discussed Brandi's post during a math class, it was only for five or ten minutes. Some of her teammates were upset by the post, but not to the level where it had a major effect on them. This was First Amendment–protected speech, SCOTUS declared. In the end, the F-bomb-dropping cheerleader scored a major First Amendment victory for kids across the country.

So, When Can Schools Punish Off-Campus Speech?

Okay, so does the *Mahanoy* SCOTUS decision mean you can take to social media and light up your school any time you're offended or annoyed by it? Not quite—SCOTUS made clear that there *are* circumstances when students could be punished for *off-campus* speech. By leaving this window open, more students and schools will get into legal battles over student off-campus speech, and with time and more court decisions, we'll know more about what the law does and doesn't consider free speech violations. For now, a school may be more likely to lawfully limit your *off-campus* speech if

- you've targeted someone specifically,

- your speech was considered a threat, or

- the post snowballed into creating a major disturbance at school.

Online Speech and Cyberbullying

It's no secret that kids spend a lot of time online: 92 percent of teenagers go online at least daily, many of them anonymously or using pseudonyms. Ever since the rise of social media, cyberbullying has been a problem for kids and teenagers. Cyberbullying is when someone threatens, harasses, intimidates, or otherwise mistreats someone else online, on social media, via email or messaging app, or by any other means using the internet.

As a student, do you see it? Have you experienced it yourself? Or perhaps you've even cyberbullied someone else? Is cyberbullying out of control? Many say—YES! In 2018, the Pew Research Center reported that a whopping 59 percent of teens had been the target of cyberbullying. That was before the Covid pandemic, when kids' and teens' lives shifted to be even more online, and there was a 70 percent increase in cyberbullying during that period.

Kids aren't on their own in combating online bullies. Parents, schools, and even lawmakers are doing their best to protect them. Currently, forty-eight states have anti-cyberbullying laws in place. Some of these laws even make it a criminal offense to bully another.

But, wait—couldn't that be considered punishing kids for their online speech and therefore violating their First Amendment rights? Even though cyberbullying involves speech, the effects of bullying are considered so bad and so dangerous for kids, that these laws have not been considered to violate free speech. Bullying has led to anxiety, depression, self-harm, and even suicide among kids and teenagers. Many of these laws allow schools to step in in cases of cyberbullying because these effects are substantial enough. While anti-cyberbullying statutes do have their First Amendment critics, most people want to see kids better protected from cruel bullying. A federal anti-bullying law has even been proposed and one day could be passed.

Are you being cyberbullied? You shouldn't be! There are laws to protect you, and more so, adults who want to help you. Tell an adult in your life. It doesn't have to be this way.

Sexting

Here's a fact that may shock you: kids can face criminal charges and fines for sexting each other. So, if you are snapping and sending off nude pics, then you could be breaking the law. Even more, the person receiving the message could face criminal charges, too. That's right—sexting is against the law in most states for minors. It doesn't matter if two people swap the photos willingly.

Even though sexting is a form of speech, when it's between underage minors, it's considered obscene and a form of child pornography—which are unprotected forms of speech under the First Amendment.

So, what counts as sexting? Sexually explicit photos, often involving partial or full nudity, transmitted by smartphone, computer, or online. It can also mean sexually explicit messages. Sexting can be between romantic partners or between friends. Sometimes people receive unwanted sexts. Sometimes kids are pressured by friends or partners to participate in sexting.

Since the rise of smartphones and social media, there have been many cases across America where high school and middle school kids have been prosecuted for sexting. These are very serious offenses. If someone is found guilty of any of these crimes, they could face punishment like a prison sentence, be known as a felon for the rest of their lives, and have to register as a sex offender. On top of that, kids who have faced sexting charges have been expelled from school and have faced difficulty in the college or job application process. This is serious stuff!

LEGAL LINGO

SEX OFFENDER REGISTRATION When someone is convicted of a sex crime, often their punishment includes being listed in a public registry as a sex offender. People can search this system, and all registered offenders are listed with information like their name, photo, home address, and past offenses.

The Internet Is Forever

A good rule of thumb before you send a text message or send a DM or post something on social media is to remember that the things you put out in the digital world can exist for years and years to come. They can potentially be accessed by anyone.

Ask yourself: Am I okay if others see this? Will I be okay if this is still online in one year, in five years, in fifty years?

Mom, Please Take Down That Photo of Me

In 2019, Goop CEO and Academy Award–winning actress Gwyneth Paltrow did something that lots of moms do: she posted a vacation photo of her and her daughter to her Instagram. Sure, most moms don't have millions of social media followers, but this kind of "sharenting" is super common. Ninety-two percent of two-year-olds have an online presence thanks to their parents' posts!

One person who didn't care for Gwyneth's post—Apple Martin, her fourteen-year-old daughter, who appeared in the photo wearing ski goggles. Apple commented for everyone to see: "Mom we have discussed this. You may not post anything without my consent." In the most mom reply ever, Gwyneth answered Apple's comment: "You can't even see your face!" But she took the photo down.

Apple stood up for herself, and her mom listened. But did Gwyneth have the right to post about her in the first place? Is the consent Apple mentioned required by law or just something that was worked out between mother and daughter?

LEGAL LINGO

CONSENT Permission to do something. When a kid says: "Yes, Dad, you can post that picture of me on Facebook," they are giving their father consent to share the photo.

Parents' or guardians' posts about their kids on social media is where parental free speech rights and kids' rights to privacy crash into one another. The bad news for kids is that your parents are entitled to this form of speech. Under the law, kids don't get to enjoy too many rights of privacy when it comes to their parents and caretakers. Their parents are their legal guardians, so, by law, they are their kids' decision makers.

It's kind of strange. When someone else or a company posts a picture of a kid without permission, your parents have the right to ask that it be taken down, and in some cases, they can even sue. But parents don't need permission from their kids to post about them. Even if it's a photo you find unflattering or embarrassing; even if it's a photo of yourself you texted to them privately; even if it's personal information that you'd rather not be out in the world; and even if it's a blog detailing every little thing that happens in your house. Although your parents most likely have good intentions, it can be frustrating that you aren't able to control your own image on the internet. Especially when you probably take such care when it comes to posting on your own social media account. If parental posting about you without your consent is not against the law, what can you do to protect your privacy online?

Guide to Convincing Your Parent to Take a Photo of You or Post About You Down

- **APPROACH THE TOPIC DELICATELY:** A good way to start the conversation would be to ask: Can I talk to you about something I'm upset about?

- **IDENTIFY THE POST(S):** Let them know which specific posts have made you uncomfortable.

- **ACKNOWLEDGE THEY DIDN'T MEAN TO RUIN YOUR LIFE:** They probably didn't mean to embarrass or upset you—they may have been coming from a place of pride or joy. You should recognize that so your parents see you are considering their perspective too. This should help make them less defensive.

- **NOTE PEOPLE WHO HAVE SEEN IT:** Identify the number of their followers who may have seen it, especially if it was shared to the open public or if it has been seen by particular people who embarrass you, like a teacher or relative or friend's parents.

o **EXPLAIN WHY IT BOTHERS YOU OR WHY IT IS HARMFUL TO YOU:** The reason could be that it embarrassed you generally or it embarrassed you in front of a certain person. Or it could be that you've been subject to bullying because of it. Perhaps it's inaccurately portraying you or perhaps you are just, generally, uncomfortable with your personal information being put out on the internet without your permission.

o **SAY THAT YOU PREFER TO KEEP PARTS OF YOUR LIFE PRIVATE AND CHOOSE TO REVEAL THEM ON YOUR OWN TERMS:** This is a hard point to argue against. Your parents probably feel the same way about their own private life.

o **SET SOME CLEAR PARAMETERS:** Perhaps you can suggest that posting family photos is okay, but not photos you text them during a private conversation without permission. Point out some of the posts they've posted in the past that you *are* okay with.

o **REMIND THEM OF THE LONG-TERM IMPACT:** Things posted on the internet stay there forever—even when you become an adult. What if you grow up and don't want posts from when you are a kid available on the internet? There are potential dangerous effects, too—posting personal information or photos of kids subjects them to increased exposure to identity fraud and online predators. Let them know if you hold these fears.

o **THANK THEM FOR HEARING YOUR POINT OF VIEW:** Remember, you're family, so try to keep things loving and civil. Keep in mind that a "thank you" can go a long way.

o **IF THEY DON'T AGREE:** One thing you could respond with is this: "I respect that is your right, but I'll be less willing to share personal things with you out of fear what you'll post online." Try revisiting the conversation again if the problem continues.

EUROPEAN UNION

The European Court of Justice has recognized a "right to be forgotten." This means that individuals have the right to have their personal information be unfindable. For kids in Europe, this means that when they grow up, it's possible to make it harder to find those old posts that may embarrass them as adults. Someone may be less excited that the TikTok dance he made in middle school is still available online when he's forty. Or that his mom's old blog posts about his "hilarious" potty-training accidents are still available for all eyes to see. In Europe, the law allows a person to request search engines like Google and Bing remove links containing personal information from search results.

STUDENT NEWSPAPER

5 Freedom of the Press

Congress shall make no law . . . abridging the freedom of . . . the press

Extra! Extra! Read all about it . . . as long as the government has reviewed and okayed it for publication. Wait—that's not right, is it? In America, the freedom of the press guaranteed in the First Amendment prevents just this kind of government behavior, censorship and punishment of reporters and journalists. In some countries, journalists who report negative news about their government—like criticizing a public official or releasing secret information—are committing a crime. They could end up in jail or have to pay steep fines. In countries where the government controls the media, typically the media is forced to paint a rosy picture of the government. Even if that picture is not so accurate. And even if the truth is that the government is responsible for doing things that many citizens are upset or angry about.

Compared to all of its sister freedoms in the First Amendment, freedom of the press is slightly different. The other rights—the right to petition, freedom of speech, freedom of assembly, and freedom of religion—are rights for all citizens. The freedom of the press clause, however, guarantees a right to a specific profession.

In 1789, "the press" meant newspapers. Today, people get their news from all kinds of sources and "the press" could mean

Magazines ○ Radio ○ Television ○ Blogs
Websites ○ Podcasts ○ Social media and more!

Why did the founders want to include a freedom for a specific profession in the First Amendment? Why the press and not other important industries? Thomas Jefferson once said, "Were it up to me to decide whether we should have a government without newspapers or newspapers without a government, I should not hesitate a moment to prefer the latter." The founders considered freedom of the press super important in creating their new, ideal country. This would not be the place for censorship or prior restraint. Instead, it would be the place where people would have a voice. It would be the place where government had to listen to its citizens. And—with freedom of the press—it would be the place where the government could get into trouble if or when it did the wrong thing.

LEGAL LINGO

CENSORSHIP Banning any kind of speech (written or spoken) because the speech is considered problematic. It can happen before or after it has been expressed. Let's say your theater class wants to put on a performance of the musical *Dear Evan Hansen*. After rehearsing for weeks, it's finally opening night. The first performance goes great—or so you think. Some parents complain that the teen suicide theme is inappropriate. You get a call from the school principal—he's made the call that the musical can no longer be performed because it could be too upsetting. You've been censored.

> **PRIOR RESTRAINT** A kind of censorship. When the government bans an expression *before* it's expressed. Your theater class is figuring out what musical they should put on this semester. You really want them to choose *Dear Evan Hansen*. But then your theater teacher hands out a list of "Forbidden Plays and Musicals" created by your principal. Right there on the list is *Dear Evan Hansen*. You can't put it on—it's been subject to prior restraint.

To Americans, freedom of the press equals access to information and truth. It also means access to differing viewpoints. A press that is not afraid of government interference or punishment is free to report on what the government is doing—whether it's good or bad, sad or happy, ugly or picture-perfect. It allows people to know about what's happening in their country and form their own opinions. This ties into the other rights provided by the First Amendment. If a citizen learns from the press that they are being treated unfairly, that citizen may be inspired to speak up and ask for change, perhaps by creating a petition or writing a letter to their congressperson or joining a protest.

Freedom of the press is also a way to keep the government in check. The media is sometimes called the "Fourth Estate," referring to the fact that it's as important as the checks and balances system laid out in the Constitution that created our three branches of government—executive, legislative, and judicial. Thomas Jefferson and the founders of the country knew that it was incredibly important that the states and their citizens had a way to keep an active and public check on the government. The press is the critical tool to do that.

Limits to Freedom of the Press

Like the other rights granted in the First Amendment, freedom of the press isn't without limits. The same limits that apply to free speech apply to the press. Two kinds of illegal speech that come up most often in journalism are defamation and invasion of privacy.

Defamation is speech that is harmful to another's reputation. For speech to be defamation, it has to be untrue. It also has to have actually caused some harm to the person, like loss of income. Also, the reporter who made the false statement either had to have done it purposefully to harm that person or hadn't been careful enough in checking their reporting. Imagine the school newspaper reports that you cheat on your history tests—but it's not true. The damage to you is real: your history teacher hands you a big, fat F grade; you get called into the principal's office for possible suspension; your parents are disappointed in you; this could go on your permanent record and maybe even affect your future college applications—plus all of your friends now think you're a cheater. The student reporter based their reporting on what only one other kid said—and that kid has had it out for you ever since that time in the fourth grade when you accidentally spilled apple juice on the front of his pants, making it look like he'd peed himself. You have a good case for defamation here. When someone is defamed in writing, it's called **libel**. When someone is defamed in spoken words, it's called **slander**. At times, both types of defamation, libel and slander, can happen at the same time. Think about the history test example above. Which form(s) of defamation do you see in the facts?

Invasion of privacy is when a media outlet reports private information about a private citizen. Private citizens have a right to keep their personal and private information from being made public. Medical history and family matters are examples of personal information. Let's say a reporter from your school newspaper reports that your parents are having big blowout fights about parenting decisions, like how much screen time you're allowed and whether you should be in trouble for your D+ in pre-algebra class. She also reports that your parents are in couples therapy and are probably going to get divorced. You feel completely wronged—your privacy was invaded. But not everyone gets the same expectations of privacy. Celebrities, public figures, and famous people don't have the same right to privacy as ordinary private people. The idea is that if you are a public person, that means you are a newsworthy person—and that makes details about your life fair game for the press and for the public to learn about them. Think about that the next time you decide you want to try to get TikTok famous! Do you think it's fair that famous people get less privacy than the rest of us? What if they didn't want or mean to become famous—what if instead they became newsworthy because they were in the right (or wrong) place at the right time or through the actions of another?

Technology and the Free Press

. . . .

It's safe to say that the drafters of the Bill of Rights weren't thinking about TikTok or Twitter when the First Amendment was created. Even though technology has changed so much about how Americans get their news, the freedom of the press envisioned by the drafters of the Bill of Rights all the way back in 1789 still holds strong.

Amazing, isn't it?

But just how bendy is the First Amendment?

Technology has definitely made things much more complicated. Let's face it—with so many sources of information bombarding your brain, it's exhausting for Americans to know which source, like Twitter or the *New York Times,* has the most accurate or truthful information. And the questions just keep coming:

- How do we fight against disinformation or "fake news" while also ensuring a free press?
- Who is considered a journalist?
- Does anyone who posts something newsworthy on their social media get the same freedom of the press protections that newspaper journalists do?

As technology and innovation progress, these are going to be bigger and bigger questions that must be figured out. This train is moving fast, and for now, it seems that no one can slow it down!

· · · · · · · · · · · · · · · · · GLOBAL PERSPECTIVE · · · · · · · · · · · · · · · · · ·

TANZANIA

During the presidency of President John Pombe Magufuli, the press in Tanzania had become seriously limited. He passed a law that doled out punishments for news reporting that was critical of the government. Newspapers and online media outlets got shut down, suspended, or fined. Journalists were also being silenced with suspensions. There was even a law making it super expensive to start a blog, making it hard for many voices to be heard.

In 2020, President Magufuli was skeptical of how bad the coronavirus pandemic was and didn't want to hear otherwise. Journalist Talib Ussi Hamad was suspended from reporting for six months for reporting on COVID-19. A local newspaper was forced to close for a while after publishing a photo of President Magufuli shopping maskless in a crowd, breaching social distancing guidelines.

Shutting down reporting of the pandemic was dangerous—Tanzanians deserved to know all the facts about COVID-19 and needed to understand its spread. They learned how serious it could be when President Magufuli died unexpectedly, supposedly from COVID-19 (although the government never admitted that). In 2021, new president Samia Suluhu Hassan decided to expand press freedom in Tanzania. She lifted bans on media organizations that had been passed under Magufuli's presidency. It seemed like a bold move in standing up for the rights of Tanzania's free press. But later that year, she quickly broke her promises to strengthen free speech and free press when her government suspended a popular independent weekly news outlet, demonstrating how fragile freedom of the press can be throughout the world.

· **GLOBAL PERSPECTIVE** ·

NORWAY

In 2021, the organization Reporters Without Borders ranked Norway as number 1 out of 180 countries in its Worldwide Press Freedom ranking. Norway takes freedom of the press and freedom of speech very seriously. One of the reasons it shines over other countries is that it has a special government commission that exists only to protect press freedom. Norway performs a yearly free speech assessment—an annual checkup to see if speech and press freedom are healthy and thriving as usual.

Kid Journalists, Student Newspapers, and Censorship

If freedom of the press applies to adult journalists, shouldn't it apply to kid journalists too? That's just the question SCOTUS was asked to answer in *Hazelwood School District v. Kuhlmeier*. In 1983, three high school students from a St. Louis, Missouri, suburb—Cathy Kuhlmeier, Leslie Smart, and Leanne Tippett—were enrolled in a journalism class. One of the cool things about this particular class was that the students got to create their own newspaper, the *Sentinel*. The three girls were editors, and they chose and managed the student staff, picked the stories they wanted to include in each issue, and edited them.

For the May 23, 1983, issue of the *Sentinel*, the students decided to include articles about teen pregnancy and the effect of divorce on kids. Among their classmates, several students were or had been pregnant and several students had divorced parents. To Cathy, Leslie, Leanne, and the rest of the *Sentinel* staff, these articles were relevant and important to them and their classmates. One of the articles, "Student Pregnancy: Three Personal Accounts," was an interview of three anonymous students about their pregnancies, where they talked about what it was like to find out they were pregnant, their parents' reactions, what being a teen mom was really like, and what they'd learned from the experience. Another article was called "Divorce's Impact Upon Kids May Have Life Long Affect [*sic*]." The reporter also interviewed students about their personal experiences. One named classmate was quoted as saying: "In the beginning I thought I caused the problem, but now I realize it wasn't me."

If these articles presented relevant issues to kids, and the student editors had gone through steps to make sources like the pregnant teens anonymous, the articles should be fit to print, right? Their principal thought otherwise. Under school policy, every issue of the *Sentinel* had to be okayed by the school principal. The day the paper was supposed to come out, the student editors noticed there was something missing—two entire pages, including their articles on divorce and pregnancy. In their classroom, their principal had left a note:

> The content of some of the articles were personal and highly sensitive—people and names were used. The information was sensitive and totally unnecessary to be included in the school newspaper. They have many other opportunities to achieve goals in journalism class or publishing of the school newspaper that do not require that kind of reporting. Learning can take place in research and reporting that is less sensitive, less controversial and certainly something that is just as beneficial to students.

In other words, the student journalists of the *Sentinel* had been censored.

"I was so mad because we had worked so hard on those articles," Cathy said. "We were trying to make a change with the school paper and not just write about school proms, football games, and piddling stuff."

To Cathy, Leslie, and Leanne, this was a violation of their First Amendment rights as journalists. They banded together and took action, filing a lawsuit against their school. From the beginning, they weren't sure how the case would go—it wasn't totally clear whether student journalists shared the same free speech rights as adult journalists, and they weren't sure how judges would decide. After losing in the lower district court but winning on appeal, the case was appealed again and was finally to be decided by the nine SCOTUS justices.

So, who won?

The school won. Unfortunately for Cathy, Leslie, and Leanne—and all student journalists—SCOTUS did not side with them. This was a huge loss for student free speech. The court made its decision based on the fact that the *Sentinel* was entirely funded by the school; that its publication was part of a class; and that the students who wrote for and edited the paper received a grade for their work. Because the paper was wholly a part of the school, everything in the paper was assumed to have the school's stamp of approval. The paper was seen as a mouthpiece for the school and the school didn't have to say anything it didn't want to. The principal had the right to make this call. SCOTUS still required that the school justify why it was limiting speech—it had to have a "reasonable relationship to legitimate educational concerns." Here, the principal laid out the school's reasons: the steps taken to protect the identities of the pregnant girls weren't enough, the divorced parents hadn't been given a chance to comment, and the topics were not appropriate, particularly for younger students. SCOTUS agreed this was enough.

The public response to the *Hazelwood* decision was huge. On one side, a lot of people, including many students, free speech organizations, advocates, and adult journalists, were completely outraged. The *Hazelwood* decision was a big blow to student journalists. They believed that kids were supposed to have the same free speech rights as adults. School was a place to learn to become a citizen, right? So then, what kind of lesson was it to diminish their citizenship rights in that very place? And if this limited free speech applied

Tips for Student Journalists

o **MAKE SURE YOUR ARTICLE IS WELL-RESEARCHED.** Practice sound journalism by fact-checking and confirming quotes.

o **MAKE SURE YOUR ARTICLE IS FAIR AND BALANCED.** Talk to both sides.

o **DON'T INCITE BAD OR ILLEGAL BEHAVIOR.** That includes violence or hatefulness toward others. A school will more likely have the right to censor an article if it causes a material disruption to students' education.

o **DON'T BE MEAN-SPIRITED.** Don't make jokes at the expense of other students or faculty.

o **AVOID OBSCENE OR LEWD LANGUAGE.** This type of language will more likely be seen as causing a disruption or being inappropriate for a school paper.

o **DON'T COPY.** Plagiarism is never okay.

o **PROOFREAD!** Perfect grammar and spelling go a long way in showing that you are taking your role as a student journalist seriously.

o **PUSH YOUR SCHOOL TO MAKE YOUR STUDENT MEDIA OUTLET A "FORUM" FOR FREE EXPRESSION.** Schools can give student media an official status that allows it broader free speech rights.

o **CONSIDER GOING INDEPENDENT.** Students who run a paper independently of their school have more freedom of speech rights. That would mean creating your very own newspaper— all you'd need is a computer to start!

to school newspapers, did it also apply to other school publications such as yearbooks, theater production books, and video productions?

Even three of the SCOTUS justices disagreed with the decision. Justice William J. Brennan Jr. wrote a scathing dissent explaining just how much he disagreed with the majority of his fellow justices. Even though it was a part of the dissent, the most quoted sentence from this case was written by Brennan: "The young men and women of Hazelwood East expected a civics lesson, but not the one the Court teaches them today."

But there were many other folks who did agree with the Supreme Court—schools should have the ability to make decisions based on legitimate educational concerns. It was also a dose of reality because adult journalists get stories killed by editors in chief all the time.

One person who was left with a bad taste in her mouth was Cathy Kuhlmeier, the layout editor for the *Sentinel* who had brought the case in the first place. She was in college when the SCOTUS decision came down. It was a huge disappointment—so disappointing that she decided to give up any dreams of being a journalist.

Even if you agreed with the court here, there's no question that under the *Hazelwood* decision, kids' free speech had become partially limited.

LEGAL LINGO

DISSENT The written opinion of a judge (or a group of judges) who disagrees with the majority, explaining all the reasons they think the other judges got it wrong and explaining how they got to their own decision.

Student Reporters
Make a Difference!

Today, there are over twelve thousand student publications in America. Student journalism is really important. School media not only creates great learning opportunities for student staff but also plays a big role in the community as a source of information for kids made by their peers. Here are just a few examples of student journalists who made an impact in their community:

- In 2007, Palo Alto, California, high school reporter Peter Johnson reported on the horrifying hazing rituals among his school sports teams. His article in the *Paly Voice* got a lot of attention and motivated his school to take action to make the school safer for its student athletes.

- In 2008, even though local media had been hesitant to investigate local gang activity, student journalists writing for the *Rampage* in Rockville, Maryland, wrote a detailed exposé, using student sources that adult journalists would not have had access to. Their coverage led to a decrease in gang-related violence, according to local police.

- When Kansas's Pittsburg High School hired a new principal in 2017, its student journalists at the *Booster Redux* decided to review her credentials. It turned out that degrees the principal claimed she had didn't exist, and some of her work history didn't add up either. The administration didn't catch these mischaracterizations, but the student journalists did. As a result, the new principal was forced to resign and the school hired a consultant to improve hiring practices.

- In 2019, after losing a classmate to suicide, the Escondido, California, students in charge of *The Chronicle* decided to focus on student mental health. They collected 370 student survey responses and presented a report on the findings, providing insight on the mental wellness of their fellow students in an article called "Invisible Wounds." Both their school and community took action based on their report, making changes to help avoid future tragedies and support student mental health.

Protecting Student Press Freedom

The fight for student press freedom continues. Efforts include the following:

o Student free speech advocates, including many students and young people, have lobbied state governments to convince their legislatures to pass "New Voices" laws that protect student journalists. These laws make it harder for schools to censor students. As of 2021, more than fourteen states have laws or administrative rules that recognize student free press rights.

o Student Press Freedom Day is a day of action that is celebrated every year to help bring attention to the importance of student journalism and a free press.

Right to Record at School

In the age of smartphones and social media, everyone has the potential to become a journalist when they post photos and videos. Sometimes people just post what's on their mind. But other times, people post the newsworthy things they see and experience. And sometimes, their posts go viral.

Fifteen-year-old Hannah Watters of Dallas, Georgia, learned what it was like to become an accidental journalist in August 2020. After months of school closures because of the COVID-19 pandemic, Hannah's North Paulding High School was reopening and she was really nervous. It felt too soon, and she worried that not enough safety precautions were being taken. Students were being encouraged, but not required, to wear masks. The school said it was "a personal choice." North Paulding offered virtual learning, but the spots had quickly filled up, so some kids like Hannah had no choice but to go back to in-person school. On her first day back, Hannah was appalled by what she witnessed. She snapped a photo of the hallway in between classes, showing her classmates packed in shoulder-to-shoulder, most not wearing masks. She posted it on Twitter. On the second day, she posted another photo of the packed hallway. Hannah's posts quickly went viral. People around the country were shocked to see the images of her school.

North Paulding High School received a lot of national media attention—and it wasn't flattering. The school released a statement defending itself, saying that the photos were taken out of context but that "there is no question that the photo does not *look* good." The school wasn't happy with Hannah for posting the photos. She was called into the office and told that she was being suspended for five days. The reasons? She had violated three school policies: using her cell phone while in school, using social media on school grounds, and posting images of minors without their permission.

Hannah was shocked. Especially because she didn't think what she had done was against the rules. High school students were excepted from the cell phone policy (that rule was directed at younger kids) and she hadn't posted the photo until the school day was over. She did admit she violated the policy of posting images of students to social media without their permission—but her classmates literally did that every day and had never gotten into trouble before. It seemed like she was being punished extra for posting photos that the school didn't like. To make matters worse, the next day, her principal came on the intercom and threatened any student found criticizing the school on social media.

Punishing a student for saying something true, accurate, and newsworthy about the school just because the school didn't like it? Does that sound like a violation of free student speech? Absolutely! First Amendment rights groups let North Paulding know what they thought of Hannah's suspension. When the school realized its response was most likely illegal under the US Constitution, it quickly reversed Hannah's suspension.

Even though some of Hannah's classmates were mad at her, she stood by her posts.

Kids are allowed to question their school's policies and whether those policies create a safe environment for them. Students have a right to report responsibly and lawfully on situations at school even if it's not flattering to the school. The power of the student press can be a powerful agent for change and an important way to keep kids safe.

Why Whistleblowers Are Important

By posting photos that showed the dangerous reality of her school's COVID-19 safety precautions (or lack thereof), Hannah Watters was doing something called whistleblowing. There is no pursing of the lips necessary in this kind of whistleblowing—Hannah was blowing the whistle on her school by alerting the public that something was wrong with its policies.

Whistleblowers are important—they help keep the government, companies, organizations, and, yes, schools in check. Whistleblowers are often people who are a part of an organization or group that identify illegal, unsafe, abnormal, or bad practices, policies, or behavior in the organization or group. They "blow the whistle" by telling a superior about the bad stuff or revealing it to the general public by posting it on a blog or social media or passing the information to a news reporter.

Because whistleblowers play such an important role in helping us be the best society we can be, free speech protects them. There are also laws that protect whistleblowers from facing punishment after they've shared the information.

Right to Record Police

In summer 2020, America erupted with rage over the murder of George Floyd by Minneapolis, Minnesota, police officer Derek Chauvin, who knelt on George's neck for a reported eight minutes and forty seconds during an arrest. George's death was seen as yet another horrifying example of police brutality against a Black person in America. Millions witnessed George's last moments after a bystander recorded and posted a video of the tragic scene. Outrage spread across the country and throughout the world. In the pandemic summer of 2020, millions of people of all backgrounds, ethnicities, cultures, languages, races, and more joined Black Lives Matter protests, making it clear that people had had enough of the inequality faced by Black people and were demanding real change.

This major social movement would never have happened if it weren't for a seventeen-year-old high school student named Darnella Frazier and her cell phone camera. Darnella and her nine-year-old cousin had been on their way to Cup Foods, the convenience store where George Floyd had been accused of passing a fake twenty-dollar bill. Just a few storefronts away, she noticed four police officers roughly handling a Black man from his car. Having witnessed Black people being treated unfairly by police before, her instincts told her she had to do something. So she stopped, pulled out her phone, and hit the record button.

"It was like a natural instinct, honestly," to start recording, she later said. "The world needed to see what I was seeing. Stuff like this happens in silence too many times." As her camera rolled, she captured George Floyd gasping for air, uttering some of his final words: "I can't breathe." These words were later emblazoned on shirts and signs at every protest, standing not just for George Floyd's death but representing the widespread systemic and institutional injustices Black people face in America.

Darnella captured the entire arrest, concluding with the officers leaving in their cars and George Floyd leaving in an ambulance, lifeless. Traumatized and horrified by what she had witnessed, Darnella knew what she had to do next: post the video on social media and let the world know about it.

During a news conference, Minneapolis police chief Medaria Arradondo said that although "we should never have to rely upon" witness video to keep police accountable, "I am thankful, absolutely, that this was captured in the manner that it was." For her exceptional courage, Darnella was given a prestigious human rights award, the 2020 PEN/Benenson Courage Award, and she also was given a special award from the Pulitzer Board, a committee that recognizes the country's best contributions to journalism.

Recording police activity is considered an act of free speech. Although SCOTUS hasn't given its official opinion yet, lower courts across the country agree that people have the right to record government officials, including police officers, while they are carrying out their duties in public. Under the First Amendment, Americans have the right to access information and to gather news. By safely recording the police while they are doing their job, citizens are helping to hold police accountable for their behavior and fight for equality.

Thanks in large part to Darnella Frazier's cell phone video, the police officers present during George Floyd's death were arrested and charged with murder. Darnella even courageously appeared as a witness in Derek Chauvin's trial. On April 20, 2021, Derek Chauvin was found guilty of

murder. Without Darnella's quick thinking, brave recording, and bold sharing of her video with the world, justice for George would not have been served. As Darnella said: "My video didn't save George Floyd, but it put his murderer away and off the streets."

What to Know When Recording the Police

Although the Supreme Court has not yet given its opinion on whether a private citizen has the right to record police, other appeals courts *have* found such a right exists and it's safe to assume that you can. Here are some things you should know:

○ **YOU ONLY HAVE THE RIGHT TO RECORD A POLICE OFFICER WHEN THEY ARE EXERCISING THEIR OFFICIAL DUTIES IN PUBLIC.** The police officer should be on duty. "In public" means a place like a street, a sidewalk, or a park. It doesn't mean a private home or store.

○ **BE SAFE.** Stay a distance away. You should not be interfering with the police activity. Your goal is to capture the moment, not be a part of the moment.

○ **BE CALM AND COURTEOUS.** This will help keep you and others safe and could help you better capture the incident.

○ **YOU CAN TAKE PHOTOS, VIDEOS, OR AUDIO.**

○ **POLICE OFFICERS CAN ORDER YOU TO MOVE OUT OF CONCERN FOR YOUR SAFETY, BUT NOT ONLY BECAUSE YOU ARE RECORDING.** For your safety, follow instructions.

> o **POLICE OFFICERS CAN ONLY SEARCH YOUR PHONE, TABLET, OR DEVICE WITH A WARRANT OBTAINED FROM A JUDGE.**
>
> o **YOU HAVE THE RIGHT TO REFUSE A REQUEST TO REVIEW OR DELETE WHAT YOU RECORDED OR TO UNLOCK YOUR PHONE OR GIVE YOUR PASSCODE.**
>
> o **YOU HAVE THE RIGHT TO POST YOUR RECORDING TO SOCIAL MEDIA.**

Adapted from Electronic Frontier Foundation.

The Censoring and Banning of Books for Kids

You walk into your school library, excited to pick up the next book in the Harry Potter series, dying to find out what happens next. You scan the shelves, but it's not there. Actually, none of the Harry Potter books are there. *I guess they must be really popular books to check out*, you think. You decide to ask the librarian for help. She informs you: "It's not on the shelves of the library and never will be. Harry Potter is on the banned books list." What?!

For decades, schools in America have banned books from their libraries, pulling books from shelves and making them inaccessible to students. Sometimes it's a school board that decides to ban certain books, or librarians or school administrators. Other times, a ban is in response to complaints by parents.

Why would they prevent kids from reading certain books? Often, their motivation comes from an earnest and good place. They think the content isn't appropriate for kids—they might even insist it's dangerous. The most common reasons given for banning books are because they contain profanity, violence, sex, sex education, homosexuality, witchcraft and the occult, "new age" philosophies, rebellious or bad-behaving kids, politically incorrect language, or racist or sexist language.

Plain and simple, banning books is a form of censorship.

And there's another problem. Not everyone agrees what's bad for kids. What some people think is "bad" content for kids, others might think is good—even necessary—content for kids. Many believe that banning kids from reading certain books limits their exposure to the vast realities of the world and denies them learning opportunities. Adults should be encouraging conversations with kids about hard topics, not avoiding them entirely.

The First Amendment guarantees that information and ideas flow freely to Americans, that many opinions and views, popular or unpopular, are accessible to everyone. Does banning books go against that? Is banning a book like banning a voice?

A group of kids from Long Island, New York, decided to find out the answer to this themselves. In 1976, members of the school board of Island Trees Union Free School District pulled nine books off of high school and junior high school library shelves, preventing students from accessing them and teachers from using them. The list of nine books was based on recommendations given at a conference attended by some of the board members, and not from actually reading the books themselves. In fact, members of the board had only read short excerpts, without any context at all. The list included classic authors like Kurt Vonnegut and Richard Wright. Troublingly, five of the nine forbidden books were written by authors of color. The reasons given for banning them? They were "anti-American, anti-Christian, anti-Semitic and just plain filthy."

Word got out to some students that the books had been banned from the library. There was an immediate uproar. Many students and parents in the community were angry that the school was banning books. Steven Pico, junior class vice president, and Russ Rieger, editor of the school paper, banded together with fellow high school students Jacqueline Gold and Glenn Yarris and junior high student Paul Sochinski. With help from the ACLU, the students filed a lawsuit against their school district. It wasn't until six years later that *Board of Education, Island Trees Union Free School District No. 26 v. Pico* finally reached SCOTUS. The court made clear that students have a right to *receive* ideas under the First Amendment. Public schools cannot remove library books "simply because they dislike ideas contained in those books." SCOTUS did add that schools had the right to ban books from the library for certain reasons—like if they were "pervasively vulgar" or not right for the curriculum. If a book is going to be removed, however, there needs to be a review of what the motivation is behind the ban. If the motivation is to deny students access to ideas that the decision maker disagrees with, it's a violation of the First Amendment.

This wasn't a slam-dunk win for students. The court was basically saying schools may have good, valid reasons to ban books. Those reasons do have to be carefully examined. This case made it harder for public schools to ban books, but it didn't make it impossible. As a result, books continue to be banned from school libraries, even today.

Some of the most frequently banned books include these:

★ *Are You There, God? It's Me, Margaret* by Judy Blume—Banned for talking about puberty and teen sexuality

★ Captain Underpants series by Dav Pilkey—Banned for offensive language, partial nudity, violence, and misbehavior

★ *George* by Alex Gina—Banned for depicting LGBTQIA+ content and not "reflecting values of our community"

★ *The Giver* by Lois Lowry—Banned for depicting death

★ Goosebumps series by R. L. Stine—Banned for being too graphic and scary for kids

★ Harry Potter series by J. K. Rowling—Banned for depicting witchcraft

★ *Heather Has Two Mommies* by Leslea Newman—Banned for depicting homosexuality

★ *Sex, Puberty, and All That Stuff: A Guide to Growing Up* by Jacqui Bailey and Jan McCafferty—Banned for talking about puberty and sex

★ *Stamped: Racism, Antiracism and You* by Jason Reynolds and Ibram X. Kendi—Banned for supporting the teaching of critical race theory

★ *To Kill a Mockingbird* by Harper Lee—Banned for racial slurs, featuring a "white savior" character, and its perception of the Black experience

★ *Walter the Farting Dog* by William Kotzwinkle and Glenn Murray—Banned for use of potty humor

★ *Where's Waldo?* by Martin Hanford—Banned for depicting a woman sunbathing topless

Banned Books Week

Since 1982, librarians, students, teachers, booksellers, publishers, and readers come together the last week of September to celebrate open and free access to books during Banned Books Week.

Check with your school or local library to see how you can participate in Banned Books Week.

You Be the Judge

In 2021, it was announced that six of Dr. Seuss's books would no longer be published because of their racist depictions of Black and Asian people in the text and illustrations. The titles included the decades-long bestsellers *And to Think I Saw It on Mulberry Street* and *If I Ran the Zoo*.

Many people were glad these stories weren't being made available to kids anymore, but many people were upset that classic books by a beloved author were being banned. We know that the First Amendment applies only to government interference and not private citizens or companies. Publishers are private companies, and so they can decide not to publish the books. But many libraries have pulled the books because of their racist and outdated imagery and words. In your opinion, is it okay for a public library or public school library to ban the books? Is their banning based on a disagreement with the books' content or something more?

6 Freedom of Assembly

> **Congress shall make no law . . . abridging . . .
> the right of the people peaceably to assemble**

What's louder than a single voice asking for change?
—A hundred voices asking for change.

What's louder than that?
—A thousand.
—A million.

So much of American history has been affected by people coming together in masses to demand change, protest injustice, and celebrate good. These kinds of group speech are protected by the First Amendment in what's called the freedom of assembly. It gives Americans the right to take to the public streets with protest signs and to march for equality and justice. In fact, this is the only First Amendment right in which more than one person is needed for it to apply. You can speak alone. You can report a story or issue alone. But can you assemble alone? Nope! There are endless possibilities on how or when or why people assemble. You can stage a sit-in or a boycott, attend a rally supporting a political candidate, celebrate an identity or heritage in a parade, or hand out flyers with information about a cause in a public square, to name a few.

The freedom of assembly is also the only First Amendment right that comes with directions: the right only exists if people assemble "peaceably." In plain words: absolutely no violence. And those assembling can't be overly disruptive to the general public. What does that mean? With few exceptions, as long as you are assembling peaceably, the government can't shut you down or punish you.

What Are Some Limits on the Right to Assemble?

o When gatherings threaten public safety and health, they can be limited.

o Curfews can be established to limit the scheduling of or time when a crowd can gather.

o Permits can be required.

o Size of a crowd can be limited.

Kids have always been a part of US protest history, using their freedom of assembly. Their voices have always been an important aspect of group speech—sometimes the most important voices. Whether they organized a social movement themselves or joined along with adults on a march, kids have helped our country evolve into a more equitable, fair, and just version of itself. And without a doubt, kids will continue that hard work.

The freedom of assembly is a bit different from the other rights in the First Amendment for one more reason. It gave birth to another right called the freedom of association. Even though it's not stated outright in the Bill of Rights, the courts realized that freedom of assembly means you also have a freedom of association—they go hand-in-hand, like the very best of friends. It means you not only have the right to peaceably assemble in groups, but the government can't stop you from associating with whomever you want, in public or in private. Whether your own parents can stop you from hanging out with certain friends—that's another story! But for the most part, the government can't stand in the way of people coming together to associate.

If you're having a hard time telling the difference, think of the freedom of assembly as your right to a one-time group thing (like a protest) and freedom of association as your right to hang out with others over a longer period of time (like joining an organization that has regular meetings).

Things that fall under the right to assemble:

o Peaceful protests in public areas

o Marches in public streets for supporting a cause

o Parades celebrating an identity like LGBTQ+ pride or a culture like Puerto Rican heritage

o Handing out pamphlets or flyers with information in public areas

o Political rallies supporting political causes or candidates

o Canvassing voters' homes to support a politician

Things that fall under the right to association:

o Meeting regularly with groups for a common cause

o Membership in a common interest group or club like the Boy Scouts

o Membership in a political party

- Membership in a sports team or club

- Membership in a church, temple, mosque, or other religious gathering place or group

- Membership in a workers' union, where workers band together to fight for better compensation, conditions, and rights

Can any or all groups just gather at any time or place for any reason? In a word—no. Just like the other freedoms protected by the First Amendment, freedom of assembly and association are not limitless. So—yes—you might find yourself squaring off with local police if you meet up with hundreds of protesters to stop animal testing and block the driveway to your public school drop-off. So—yes—you might find yourself being arrested or detained if you block access to Times Square in the middle of rush hour. It would be chaos if groups of people could just gather anywhere at any time of day to spread their message. New York City would be a mess. Or, what if you're in a group that decides to stage a parade that plays loud music at four a.m. on a Tuesday? Would streaming by hospitals, nursing homes, and private homes filled with sleeping families who need to go to school and work in the morning go over well with local officials? There would be a lot of very cranky, tired people.

The government can regulate three things when it comes to public assembly: time, place, and manner—but never the content. Here are some examples:

- TIME: A protest is allowed to take place during daylight hours.

- PLACE: A protest is permitted in a public park, but not on a well-trafficked public street.

- MANNER: A protest must be nonviolent.

To be able to regulate these factors, the government has to have really good reasons. These reasons are often practical—for example, avoiding blocking traffic, preventing too much noise or litter, and avoiding destruction of private homes and properties. A city or town can require a group to obtain a permit before it can stage a protest or a parade.

An Unpeaceable Assembly

On August 12, 2017, hundreds of protesters from far-right groups participated in a "Unite the Right" rally in Charlottesville, Virginia. The permitted rally brought together many different hate groups like neo-Nazis, the Klansmen, white nationalists, and neo-fascists who were passionate about their anti-Semitic, anti-Islam, anti-immigrant views, as well as the Confederate flag. They had gathered not just to unite groups with common ground, they also opposed the city's removal of a statue of Robert E. Lee, the general who led the South's Confederate forces during the Civil War.

Many counter-protesters were also there to let the far-right groups know they didn't agree with their views.

Things got very ugly very fast. Just two hours after the day's protest officially began, with shouts of "Jews will not replace us" and "white lives matter" echoing in downtown Charlottesville, violence broke out between the protesters and counter-protesters. Violence filled the streets and got so bad that the city revoked the Unite the Right rally permit and declared it an unlawful assembly.

But the violence went on. The protest turned tragic when a car driven by an Unite the Right rally participant plowed into counter-protesters, killing a young woman named Heather Heyer. Later that afternoon, two policemen were killed when their helicopter crashed on the way to help maintain peace at the event. This is a case of a permitted protest turned unpeaceable, and therefore, it's not protected by the First Amendment. What's more, violent participants faced arrest and criminal prosecution.

You Be the Judge

On January 6, 2021, thousands gathered on the National Mall in Washington, DC, protesting President Donald Trump's defeat in the 2020 presidential election to Joe Biden. Despite having required permits, the protest turned unpeaceable and illegal once violence ensued—mostly against the Capitol Police—and protesters breached the Capitol building. Protesters climbed the stairs and burst into the building that contained US congresspeople, senators, and Vice President Michael Pence at work affirming the election results. It took hours to secure the building, after 140 people were injured. As a result of the day, five people died during or shortly after the riot. The Capitol building hadn't seen such an attack since the War of 1812.

It's important to note that most of the rioters were not arrested during or directly after the assault on the Capitol on or around the National Mall. Although hundreds of arrests followed in the weeks and months after the assault on the Capitol and many participants were prosecuted and handed jail sentences, the majority of violent rioters were allowed to leave freely. Given everyone gets the same treatment no matter their message, many Americans have questioned how race may have played a major factor in how these violent rioters, who some call insurrectionists, were allowed to easily enter the Capitol building, and even attack and cause the deaths of Capitol Police and other protesters, and simply walk away that very night free and unharmed. In contrast, six months earlier, in many cities, thousands of mostly peaceful, unarmed Black Lives Matter protesters were met with tear gas and rubber bullets in our nation's capital—directly across from the White House. Does it seem everyone really gets the same treatment when exercising the "right of the people peaceably to assemble"? Close your eyes and imagine if there were Black and brown faces with weapons beating up Capitol Police and breaking into the Capitol building on January 6. Do you think the immediate response from authorities would have been the same? What are ways in which people can use their First Amendment rights to highlight this kind of unfair treatment?

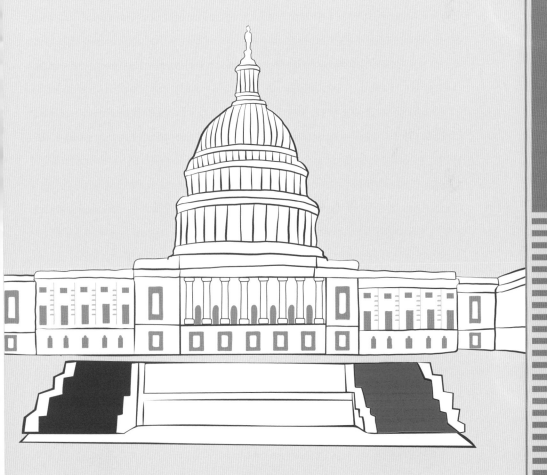

GLOBAL PERSPECTIVE

GERMANY

Under its Youth Protection Act, Germany has established lots of rules for when and where kids can assemble. For example, kids under the age of sixteen can't go to a restaurant or café unaccompanied by a parent or guardian. Any kid under sixteen can't be alone at a movie theater after ten p.m. What happens if kids get caught in the wrong place after hours? They don't get punished under the law, but their parents do!

Kids' Protests in History

Public protest is an important part of the story of America and much of that protest history involves youth activists. Since the early days of our Union, brave kids have found the courage to speak up, make their voices heard, and fight for change, equality, and fairness. These are some of their stories.

THE NEWSBOYS STRIKE OF 1899

In America's early days, kids from working-class and poor families didn't go to school—they went to work. Many states had minimum age laws so that children had to be at least a certain age (like twelve years old) to work, but many parents sent their kids to factories, mills, farms, shops, or other people's homes at a much younger age, lying about how old they actually were. Families needed to eat, they needed clothes, they needed shelter, and every able body had to help out. Sometimes kids as young as six were put to work.

Many industries thrived on child labor. Some employers preferred child laborers because they could pay them cheaply and their small bodies were well suited for certain jobs like cleaning intricate machinery. Kids worked long hours and were subject to dangerous conditions that too often resulted in injuries, illnesses, or worse. It's hard to imagine young kids being put to work like this today and that is the result of many decades of protests, lobbying, and fighting—led by both adults and kids—for the fair treatment of child laborers. Eventually, harsh child labor conditions were abolished entirely.

History's path to justice for child workers includes the Newsboys Strike of 1899 in New York City. In cities across the country, newspapers were sold by young kids, mostly boys between the ages of eleven and fifteen who represented nearly every ethnic and racial group. These "newsies" walked the streets hawking the morning, afternoon, and evening editions, shouting out

Kid Protester Hall of Fame 1835–1925

HARRIET HANSON

Lowell Mill Workers Strike | Lowell, Massachusetts, 1836

At eleven years old, Harriet Hanson worked at a cloth mill as a "bobbin girl" whose job was to handle the machinery and replace spools of yarn called bobbins. Like most of her coworkers, she lived at the mill's boardinghouse. When factory owners raised the cost of living without increasing factory workers' wages, the young, female mill workers decided to strike. When the first day of the strike arrived, the girls in Harriet's room hesitated, fearful of the consequences of their actions. But young Harriet said, "I don't care what you do. I'm going to turn out, whether anyone else does or not." She led the way out of the room, and the others followed. Although this strike wasn't entirely successful, it inspired other work strikes that ultimately resulted in better working conditions for kids. Harriet went on to become a suffragette who fought for women's right to vote.

DOROTHY FROOKS

··

Women's Suffrage Movement | Bayonne, New Jersey, 1910

At age eleven, Dorothy Frooks parked herself on the street corners of Bayonne, New Jersey, captivating large crowds with the charismatic way she talked about women's right to vote. The newspaper recognized her as one of the best speech-givers around. She enlisted schoolchildren across the city in supporting women's suffrage. By age fifteen, she was the president of Bayonne's chapter of the Equal Justice League for Women's Votes. Dorothy grew up to see women gain the right to vote and became a lawyer and an author.

THE CHILDREN'S CRUSADE, BIRMINGHAM, ALABAMA, 1963

If you were Black and living in the American South in the 1960s, injustice invaded so many parts of your existence. That was especially true in Birmingham, Alabama, where racial prejudice was not only prevalent in its people but the city's government encouraged it. Although SCOTUS had issued its decision to desegregate schools in *Brown v. Board of Education*, the white leaders of Birmingham refused to integrate the Black and white students of their schools. Black students weren't being given the same quality of education as white students, with worse facilities and supplies. And segregation existed in many places outside of school in Birmingham—Black kids weren't allowed to share the same swimming pools or water fountains as white kids; Black people couldn't sit in certain areas of restaurants or buses. When the circus came to town, Black kids weren't welcome. Black workers were paid less than their white peers. Even worse, racially motivated violence was happening in the streets, including the bombings of Black homes and churches. It was absolutely clear that Black people were not being treated fairly or equally to white people—but Birmingham's white-only leaders were not interested in equality.

The Black community of Birmingham had had enough of being treated this way and having to explain to their children the realities of their grim world. Things had to get better, but it seemed only they could help themselves. Many staged protests and many were jailed as a result, including Dr. Martin Luther King Jr. From his cell, he famously wrote his *Letter from Birmingham Jail* where he called on people to break unjust laws in order to force change.

After his release, Dr. King and many Black citizens of Birmingham gathered at a church to discuss what their next steps should be in their fight for equality. Too many adults were spending time protesting or in jail when they needed to be working and providing for their families. How could the community protest injustice but keep their families safe and provided for? A new idea was birthed—what if the children marched instead? What would happen if the city had to fill their jails with children?

This was a scary thought. No one wanted their kids in harm's way. The adults hesitated, but the cause was important. This was for equality. Black people couldn't live this way anymore. And the young Black population of Birmingham was more than willing to help. Many high school and middle school students quickly volunteered to take part in a protest, knowing they would likely have to go to jail. Even elementary school students joined in the effort. One of the youngest marchers, Audrey Hicks, was only nine years old. After attending the church planning meeting, she told her parents she wanted to be arrested. Her parents were nervous, but Audrey was brave and this was important work, so they agreed.

At eleven a.m. on May 2, 1963, a day called Demonstration Day, or D-Day, about one thousand anxious but eager students gathered at the Sixteenth Street Baptist Church, the starting place of their march to City Hall. Audrey looked around and didn't see anyone from her elementary school—she was the only one. Knowing she would probably go to jail for a few days, her parents armed her with a board game so that she would have a way to spend the time. With their parents watching on the sidewalks, the Black youth of Birmingham started their march for equality.

That first day, 970 students were arrested for parading without a permit, including Audrey. As her parents watched, little Audrey was led into the paddy wagon with the other students. She was then booked at the jail and put in a cell. The jail was packed with older kids. Even though she didn't have anyone her age to play with, she had her game. The students also sang protest songs together, like "We Shall Overcome." Her mother, who knew someone at the jail, called to make sure her Audrey was safe.

The second day of the march brought violence. The Birmingham police force didn't seem to care that the marchers were just kids. They pointed powerful water hoses at them, soaking and injuring them. Children linked arms, but the torrents of water whipped at them and dragged them to the ground. German shepherd dogs were unleashed on them. But still, the children marched peaceably. On the second day, hundreds more children were arrested. The jails of Birmingham were filling up fast, often with sopping wet and injured kids. Some kids were brought to alternative sites like the pigpens at the city fairgrounds.

On the third day, undeterred by the near certainty of police violence, thousands more kids and teens showed up. The Birmingham police force didn't relent either, bringing their water hoses and dogs and continuing to make arrests. At a rally that evening, inspired by the children, Dr. King reassured the crowd that the children were alright and said: "Don't hold them back if they want to go to jail, for they are doing a job for all of America, and for all of mankind." Children continued to show up in Birmingham's streets and the protests forged on.

As news of the march hit national and international media, people across the country and the world were disgusted and horrified by the photos and footage they saw of children being brutalized at the hands of Birmingham authorities. The images were shocking and the bravery of the children stunning. What drove these children to willingly endure such hardship? The ugly realities of life in Birmingham for Black people—and across the American South—were now being understood on a wide scale. *This isn't right*, many people realized for the first time.

The public's outrage reached the White House. President John F. Kennedy was also deeply troubled by the images he was seeing and reports he was getting out of Birmingham. America's shame was now unveiled to the entire world.

After eight days and after thousands of children marched for justice, the city of Birmingham buckled under the pressure of the fury directed at it from across the country. Birmingham officials realized there was no choice but to make changes. Dr. King reached an agreement with the white leaders of Birmingham. The more than two thousand jailed children would be released and the city would begin desegregation with some important first steps, like allowing all restrooms and water fountains to be shared by Black and white people alike, allowing Black people to sit at restaurant counters, and making real efforts at job equality. It wasn't a complete solution, but it was a really good start.

As for Audrey, she spent an entire week in a juvenile hall jail. She didn't have a change of clothes, slept in an iron bed, ate some gross food, and missed her parents, but she had her game, her fellow marchers, and the understanding that what was she was doing was important.

When Audrey was released, she was happy to be reunited with her proud parents. The very next day, she went right back to school. Audrey's days as a brave young pioneer weren't over. She went on to volunteer to integrate a school, being one of the first Black students at a school that previously allowed only white students.

Although America's struggle with equality for Black people remained far from over, Audrey and the other children who marched together, demanding justice, captured the hearts and attention of the world. They had accomplished what their parents couldn't do: have people understand that what was happening in Birmingham wasn't right and that it had to change. The Birmingham children didn't just inspire change in their own city, they motivated people to fight for equality across the country. President Kennedy was previously hesitant to create federal laws helping to protect Black people from unfair treatment, but with his eyes open to the realities of racism in America, he decided the federal government needed to do something and, in June, he proposed the first federal civil rights legislation that ultimately resulted in the Civil Rights Act of 1964. These brave and passionate children helped fuel the Civil Rights Movement and pave the way to the most important piece of legislation related to equality in American history.

Kid Activist Hall of Fame 1926–1999

LORRAINE AGTANG

Delano Grape Strike | Delano, California, 1965–1970

Filipino Mexican American Lorraine Agtang and her family worked in the fields of Chamorro Farms in Delano, California, picking grapes. When their pay was cut from $1.40 per hour to $1.25 per hour, Lorraine, along with the rest of her family, walked off the fields in protest. Twelve days later, Cesar Chavez and more than 1,200 Mexican workers joined the strike that developed into a five-year battle with grape growers for fairer treatment, which ultimately resulted in victory for the farm workers. Lorraine was one of the only female strikers and one of the youngest. Outside of Sacramento's City Hall is a bronze memorial depicting Chavez leading two dozen protesters on a march for justice, including one thirteen-year-old girl—Lorraine.

GAY INTERNATIONAL YOUTH SOCIETY OF GEORGE WASHINGTON HIGH SCHOOL

LGBTQ+ Rights Movement | New York, New York, 1972

The very first student club for LGBTQ+ kids was formed at George Washington High School in the Washington Heights neighborhood of Manhattan. It was started by a group of BIPOC students and paved the way for a wave of gay-straight alliance and gender-sexuality alliance groups in schools, now a staple across America. These students demanded their right to exist, to be heard, and to be treated fairly.

JENNIFER KEELAN

· ·

Capitol Crawl for Disability Rights | Washington, DC, 1990

Born with cerebral palsy, eight-year-old Jennifer Keelan left her wheelchair at the bottom of the steps of the US Capitol Building and crawled her way up to the top in a demonstration showing the importance of accessibility to those with disabilities. The Capitol Crawl is considered one of the final pushes Congress needed to pass the Americans with Disabilities Act, a hugely important law that guarantees more accessibility and rights to Americans with disabilities.

THE STUDENTS OF MARJORY STONEMAN DOUGLAS HIGH SCHOOL AND THE MARCH FOR OUR LIVES

A 2:21 p.m. on February 14, 2018, the unimaginable happened at Marjory Stoneman Douglas High School in Parkland, Florida. A former student entered one of the school's buildings armed with a semiautomatic gun and opened fire for six minutes on the people inside. Seventeen people died and seventeen more were injured. Most of them were freshman students; the youngest victims were just fourteen years old. It is the deadliest high school mass shooting in US history.

For years, school shootings had plagued America. No age group of students was safe—college, high school, middle school; even elementary schools had been targeted by shooters. Students had heard lawmakers deliver their "thoughts and prayers" time and time again—but no action. Gun rights remained broad, regulations that seemed like common sense to many Americans—like background checks and bans on assault rifles—never made it through state legislatures or Congress. The opposing force was too powerful. Many pro-gun lawmakers, often financially supported by the National Rifle Association (NRA), believed they were protecting the Second

Amendment, stating they didn't think such measures would result in safer schools. To many students across America, it seemed adults valued guns more than their lives.

The shooting stirred something inside the surviving Stoneman Douglas students. Although they were still mourning the loss of their friends, classmates, siblings, and school staff, there was also anger—and that anger inspired activism. Senior David Hogg, a passionate journalism student and local newspaper intern, had pulled out his phone while he and his classmates were hiding from the shooter in a classroom closet. He recorded what was happening, reporting on what he and his classmates witnessed. He didn't stop there. That night, he was interviewed on national news, not only describing the horrors that he and his classmates had witnessed but also directly blaming the lack of stricter gun laws. His poise and conviction impressed many, and David was interviewed again and again, each time his message getting clearer and stronger—enough was enough. Gun control legislation was needed now.

In the aftermath of the shooting, junior class president Jaclyn Corin didn't think posting on social media like her classmates were doing was enough. She knew she needed to be interacting with people who could actually do something to make change. Something had to be done to wake up state legislators and make them see the dangers kids faced in schools because of lax gun laws. She was good at organizing things and decided she would lead a group of Douglas students on a trip to the state capitol in Tallahassee to meet with state leaders. Very quickly, Jaclyn had a group of a hundred kids ready to make the trek.

Meanwhile, junior and self-described "theater kid" Cameron Kasky and a group of other Douglas students gathered to talk about what action they could take to actually prevent an atrocity like they experienced from happening again. First, they started a #neveragain hashtag campaign and started social media accounts for their new group. Finally, inspired by the Women's March of 2017, they came up with a big idea: a march on Washington.

In the days after the shooting, many Douglas students found their voices and used them to speak up and tell adults more needed to be done to stop gun violence and to keep kids safe. One of those students was senior Emma Gonzalez. Emma transfixed the world when the shaved-headed, bright-eyed student delivered a passionate rally speech telling the adults in government just what they thought about their inaction: "The people in the government are lying to us. And us kids seem to be the only ones who notice and are prepared to call B.S." The speech quickly went viral and the world realized that these kids from Parkland meant business and they weren't going anywhere.

Although David, Jaclyn, Cameron, and Emma's efforts started separately, they quickly came together, knowing their message was more impactful if they acted as a unified force. Together, their voices were stronger. And they knew there were thousands more kids who would join them.

Just days after a mass murderer showed up at their school, the students announced their march on Washington, which they had given a powerful name: the March for Our Lives. This was a movement *for* kids *by* kids. They called on children and teens across the country to join them, to join their voices together so that state and federal legislatures would hear them loud and clear: kids want to be safe and that means passing better gun laws.

The March for Our Lives was an important part of their movement, but by no means was it the only part. The Douglas students honored victims in vigils, used social media to spread their gun control message, organized rallies in Florida as well as a national student walkout, took Jaclyn's trip to Tallahassee to talk to state lawmakers, sent a group to Washington to talk to federal lawmakers, and even partook in a televised town hall with President Donald Trump.

The kids were determined and were totally unified in their message: something needs to be done about gun violence now. This wasn't a small bit of activism; they were leading a movement. As politicians gave answers that seemed insufficient or hypocritical, people across the country—especially kids—took notice. The movement was growing.

To pull off their march, the Parkland kids needed money. Soon after announcing their march, they received donations from unexpected sources—actor George Clooney and his human rights lawyer wife Amal, Oprah Winfrey, director Steven Spielberg and his wife Kate Capshaw, and film producer Jeffrey Katzenberg and his wife Marilyn donated to the cause, on top of eighteen thousand other individual donations from across the country. David, Cameron, Emma, Jaclyn, and their friends soon had over $2 million to fund the March for Our Lives.

The Parkland kids knew they represented only part of the population in America—they were mostly upper-middle-class white students. Gun violence was a problem across America, and it wasn't just schools but communities that faced gun violence every day. They reached out to youth anti–gun violence groups from cities like Chicago and Los Angeles and included them in their efforts.

As the march approached, the Parkland kids faced backlash. Pro-gun advocates criticized them, mocked them, even threatened them. All of this even though they were children and even though they were victims of a

recent mass shooting at their school. But the Parkland students were unde-terred. Their mission was too important, the need for change too immediate.

On March 24, the March for Our Lives took place in Washington, DC. Hundreds of thousands of people showed up, many of them kids and teenagers. Sister marches in eight hundred towns and cities across the globe were held. It was one of the biggest youth-led rallies in American history. David, Cameron, Jaclyn, Emma, and other student activists from Parkland and across the country spoke to the crowds, including Martin Luther King Jr.'s nine-year-old granddaughter, Yolanda Renee King. The rally featured performances by singer and actress Jennifer Hudson, who lost family members to gun violence, as well as Ariana Grande, Demi Lovato, Miley Cyrus, and Common, among others. It was nationally televised for the world to see.

The March for Our Lives was a huge success in terms of getting kids across the country unified and their message out. But the Parkland student activists didn't stop there. After school let out (because, yes, they were still going to school during all of this), they spent the summer crisscrossing the country on a bus tour, speaking with kids and registering students to vote, encouraging them to use their power as young voters to elect pro–gun legis-lation leaders.

Although gun control laws remain a very hard-fought issue in the United States, the impact of the Parkland students is clear. After the March for Our Lives, states across the country passed at least fifty gun control laws. This included their own state of Florida, in a law named for them: the Marjory Stoneman Douglas High School Public Safety Act. Importantly, they invig-orated a whole generation of kids to speak up against the failures of adults to protect them, encouraging thousands to register to vote and elect leaders who will take gun control seriously. The fight is not over. The Parkland stu-dents continue their fight to eliminate gun violence in America.

INTERNATIONAL INDIGENOUS YOUTH COUNCIL

Dakota Access Pipeline Protests | Standing Rock Indian Reservation, North Dakota and South Dakota, 2016

When Energy Transfer Partners announced it intended to install an oil pipeline beneath the Missouri River, the main source of drinking water for the Standing Rock Sioux reservation, a group of Native American youth decided to take action. Not only would the pipeline damage drinking water and the environment, but it could also destroy ancient Sioux burial grounds and cultural sites. The first thing the group did was set up a prayer camp on the reservation. Next, to bring more attention to their cause, they organized relay runs from the reservation to Washington, DC, to bring the government's attention to their concerns. Eventually, thousands of indigenous people across many tribal nations joined the prayer camp and participated in their runs for clean water. Even more people gathered to protest the Dakota Access Pipeline, attracting national media and the attention of President Barack Obama. Eventually, the pipeline project was stopped. Even when President Donald Trump revived it, it was halted again in court and finally killed for good in 2021 under President Joe Biden. The IIYC continues their fight for clean water and the preservation of Native culture and traditions.

JEROME FOSTER II

Climate Change | Washington, DC

After learning about climate change at five years old, Jerome Foster II wondered why more wasn't being done about it. Two years later, he attended his first rally and his passion for environmental activism was ignited. Starting when he was sixteen, Jerome protested in front of the White House and Harvard University for over eighty consecutive weeks, demanding more action to counteract climate change. He did this in answer to youth climate change activist Greta Thunberg's Fridays for Future movement. Jerome didn't stop there: he founded a climate-focused journal and nonprofit group and helped organize some of the top climate marches in Washington, like the Global Climate Strike, which attracted millions of youth protesters worldwide, including thousands in Washington, DC.

THANDIWEH ABDULLAH

Black Lives Matter | Los Angeles, California

Born to activists and a niece of a Black Lives Matter movement cofounder, Thandiweh Abdullah grew up understanding the power of social activism. In 2015, Thandiweh helped found the Black Lives Matter Youth Vanguard, a group standing up for the rights of Black children. Thandiweh and the BLM Youth Vanguard have helped to remove random searches at schools in the Los Angeles Unified School District. Their ultimate goal is to get rid of school police from campuses entirely, making schools safer for Black students.

JEROME FOSTER II

Tell me about where your passion for activism for combating climate change came from.

It wasn't really one spark. But it was a series of moments of empathy. People ask me—Have you been directly impacted by a natural disaster? Have you been in the midst of the climate crisis? I say—no! Because I'm in Washington, DC, I have not been in a tornado, wildfire, or flooding, BUT I have the empathy as a young person and know that I must advocate on behalf of those that aren't here. One of the first signs that I made was: "I speak for that which cannot speak against those who do unspeakable things."

My original passion and how I got into climate was mostly astrophysics. I went from learning about the world around me to learning about what my own planet is like. That led me into environmentalism by having a deep love for space, and then, turning it back on my own planet.

As I got older, I understood the scale, scope, and speed of the climate crisis through reading books, watching documentaries, and having conversations with my mother and father about it.

The narrative before youth came into the climate movement was that no one really cares about this. This is only about polar bears and melting glaciers. It changed because after we started climate striking, after we started organizing in massive numbers, it became very clear—it wasn't that no one cared. No one had the ability to show that they cared. It was to show the scale of our concern in a unified way. It allowed us to come together and say this is a generation-wide call to action for people to actually take this seriously and act in the emergency capacity that this is.

What was one of your most eye-opening experiences that inspires your activism?

> A trip to Iceland was transformative. We had been on the glacier for about five hours—doing research. When we came back, the path that we took had melted. We had to go around, we had to divert. In those five hours, it was melting right in front of our eyes.

You've been named an Environmental Justice Advisory Council Member by the White House. Very few people in the United States will ever get to step inside the White House, much less be invited to pull up a chair and help make pivotal decisions that impact our nation. How did you get there and what is that experience like?

> I founded an organization called OneMillionOfUs, which rallied one million young people to register and turn out to vote in the 2020 election. I founded that with two of my fellow interns from Congressman John Lewis's office to create a space where all the major youth social movements would come together—climate justice, immigration reform, gender equality, racial equality, LGBTQ+ rights, and gun violence prevention. They all come together and fight for the fact that we need equitable justice in every aspect of our lives.
>
> After that, we organized through social media, through so many different means to create what we called "PROM AT THE POLLS" since the Class of 2020 didn't have a prom. We said that we're going to redo our prom but have it happen on November 3, Election Day, and have our prom mean more than just graduating into adulthood but graduating into becoming a first-time voter. After that, we were trying to figure out what happens next and I got a call in early February that the White House wanted me to join to be a part of the White House Environmental Justice Advisory Council, which oversees 40 percent of executive funds, making that money go to Black and brown communities that are not being prioritized by the climate crisis. We make sure that we write executive orders that are equitable and prioritize environmental justice.

I was ready to shake things up. I was like—we need money right now, we need to fix these problems right now. And it was hard understanding the reality of how slow government is and how much compromises you have to make. It was good getting into the room, but realizing that—people are ignoring you in other ways. I am always the one pushing for more progressive issues; everyone else is in their fifties and sixties. It's hard being a nineteen-year-old saying that "This is the scale of action that needs to be taken."

If you were to give a tutorial on using one's right to assembly, what would you say? How would you tell kids how to take action?

I think you have to start with empathy, and if you start with the core idea of: I'm fighting for what I am concerned about. You figure out what is in the scope of your power. If you're in Colorado, it may look different than Washington, DC. Because I lived in DC, I was able to go out and organize because I knew protests were happening every single day in DC. If you are pure in your intent and pure in what you are fighting for, it always leads you in the right way. There have been so many turns and pivots that I've made—from technology to blogging to more formal-style journalism to activism. Just start wherever you can. You may think the only thing you can do is, like, a poster or sign a petition, but there are so many things! Think: "This one action is not my only power."

Do you think it's fair that your generation has to take on climate change?

No. I think it's totally just really wrong.

What Public Protesters Should Know

o Your right to protest is strongest in public places like streets, parks, and sidewalks. You can also protest outside of government buildings, like a town or city hall, but cannot block government employees from accessing the building or keep them from conducting their work.

o You can bring signs, wear messages on your clothes, chant, shout, and sing about your cause.

o On public property, you can photograph and video record anything in public view, including police activity. This is not true if you are on private property.

o You can't be detained by police unless there is reasonable suspicion you've committed a crime.

o A city or town may require a permit for a protest.

o Counter-protesters are allowed to protest.

o Don't get violent with counter-protesters, authorities, or anyone.

o Police can ask you to do things for safety reasons, like move to one side of the street to allow traffic.

STEP 1

STEP 2

STEP 3

7 The Right to Petition

> **Congress shall make no law . . . abridging . . .
> the right of the people . . . to petition the
> government for a redress of grievances**

Last but certainly not least, the First Amendment grants all Americans the right to petition. Out of all the freedoms, the right to petition is probably the one that is least talked about and most overlooked. Think of the right to petition as the reliable older sibling to the other four louder, rowdier, flashier brother and sister freedoms. He may not be the life of the party, but you can count on him to show up with a great gift.

So, what does it mean exactly to petition the government? And "redress of grievances" sounds pretty serious, doesn't it? Well, simply put, to petition means to ask someone to do something. The Petition Clause (as this part of the First Amendment is called) guarantees citizens the right to ask their government *to do* something, *to change* something, *to take action* in order to remedy (aka redress!) a problem or a complaint (aka grievances!).

LEGAL LINGO

REDRESS To set something right after you or something have been wronged. If you accidentally knock your friend's french fries to the ground at lunchtime, the redress would be to give her your own fries or buy her some more.

GRIEVANCE A statement of complaint based on something unfair or wrong. After having her fries knocked to the ground, your friend's grievance might be: "Hey! Why'd you do that? Now I don't have fries to eat! That's not fair!"

Guess what? Americans can't be punished for making requests for change.

Citizens are absolutely allowed to petition anyone or any part of the government. That includes your individual congresspeople, senators, Congress as a whole, courts, administrative agencies, members of the executive branch— even the president. You can petition them at any time!

Under the right to petition, Americans can do the following:

o Write a letter

o Send an email

o Post a social media message

o Start or sign an online petition

o Start or sign a paper petition

o File a lawsuit

o Lobby members of Congress or government officials

You may have heard of a "petition" before. Petitioning is not just an act, it's an actual thing. A formal petition is a collection of real signatures from real people who all feel the same way about a certain real issue. It's usually all about pushing for change.

We all know a kid can't vote or drive a car or enter into a contract without their parents' approval. But do you know whether a kid can sign a petition? Yes! Absolutely! The federal government requires anyone who starts or signs a petition on their website to be at least thirteen years old. Not only can you *sign* a petition if you've reached teendom, but you can also *start* your own petition.

Just keep in mind—simply because you have the right to ask the government to do something doesn't mean it has to do it—and it actually doesn't even have to respond. Wait, what? Isn't that blatantly unfair to go through the full-blown effort of making a written request after gathering support and lots of signatures only for the government to blow it off? Well, think about how tough it would be for the US government to keep up with every single request for action. Some petitions are made seriously, but some are not. The range of petitions could be from: "There are no ramps in the public libraries in my state and people with disabilities must be given the same access as able-bodied people" to "I want my pet snake to be allowed to go to school with me" and everything in between! It would take too much time and money for the government to respond to every single request.

With petitions, think—loud. So, short of scribbling "LOOK AT ME, PRETTY PLEASE!" in bold red ink at the top of each page, how do you get the government to notice your petition? One way is to join your single voice with many other voices. If others want to make the same request you do, then unite! That makes your petition even stronger. It's harder for the government to ignore when so many citizens care about the same issue. Think about it this way: Why are fire alarms loud? So we can hear them, right? What does the loud noise do? It causes us to take it seriously and react immediately. Keep that same formula when thinking about creating a petition. Which is louder—a single voice or a large group shouting one message? Which will cause the audience—in this case, the government—to take it more seriously and react?

Also, think impact. Even if you don't get a direct response or commitment to action, your petition could still be impactful. Sure, the ultimate sign of success is if the government takes direct action based on what you asked for, especially in the way you asked for it. But there are other measures of success when it comes to petitions. First of all, with your work to make a difference in your community—your civic engagement—you've gotten the word out on a super important issue. That could lead to more people caring about the issue you raised, making it more likely that others take action to help in the future. Government officials may not have replied to your single petition, but perhaps they've read it, seen the public support, and are now aware of the issue, will be thinking about it, and might even take action later on. You've gotten the ball rolling on change. This petition didn't work this time, but maybe the next one will.

Petitioning Was Once the Popular Kid

When the Bill of Rights was being created by our Founding Fathers, there wasn't too much debate about whether there should be a right to petition—as if it was a given that it should be in the First Amendment along with the other rights. It helped that it was already a right included in many state constitutions. Petitioning had already been super popular in pre-Constitution colonial America. In those days, there was no internet, social media messenger, or even any fast and reliable snail mail—information just traveled way slower, if at all.

If you were a citizen and you wanted to alert your government to the fact that, say, something was just plain unfair, the best way to do that was to inform them yourself by filing a petition. And the government relied on being informed of problems and issues by citizens' petitions. In this era, a petition looked more like what we think of as a lawsuit, where the wronged party (the plaintiff) sues the party they think wronged them (the defendant) to help right the wrong. In colonial America, this petition was your big chance to inform and persuade the government of your problem or position. And believe it or not, for a long time, colonies' governmental bodies actually responded to almost every petition with a formal investigation, a finding, and a decision that was put into the public record. Regular people even introduced their own bills that could be turned into law. In fact, during this era, more laws were created on the basis of petitions than anything else! At the time, petitions were the primary tool to create change.

Even in colonial times, this right to petition was available to everyone, even people who didn't have the right to vote (remember, only landowning white men had the right to vote), including women, Native Americans, foreign-born citizens, formerly and currently enslaved people, and, yes, kids. That's right: they all actively used their voice to petition the government to hear their calls for change!

Over time, the way people petitioned changed drastically. Once the nation was officially formed and the government established, Congress couldn't answer every petition anymore—there were just too many and they had lots of other important things to do. So, Congress started directing petitioners to federal agencies instead. Or, in some instances, didn't answer them at all.

Some of the petitions Congress chose to ignore were important ones. In 1830, a petition was filed by a group that included early female activists Harriet Beecher Stowe and Angela Grimke, asking Congress not to remove members of the Cherokee tribe from their native lands. The petition went unanswered, and the Cherokees were kicked out of their home in a tragic historical moment now known as the Trail of Tears. Later in that same decade, many antislavery groups called abolitionists filed petitions with Congress related to ending slavery in the South. They used this tool to try pressuring the government to free enslaved men and women and end this horrifying practice once and for all. Buckling under pressure from southern states, Congress established a "gag rule" in 1840—it wouldn't review any petitions related to ending slavery at all. The House of Representatives declared that absolutely no petitions "praying the abolition of slavery . . . shall be received by this House, or entertained in any way whatsoever." This is another shameful example of a moment when early leaders could have changed the course of history for America's enslaved people, but decided against it. This sorry episode also solidified the idea that the right to petition in the First Amendment was just a right to be heard, not a right to a full hearing on the issue raised.

Following this gag rule and Congress's unwillingness to decide on every petition—even important ones—the lawsuit petition format became less popular. People realized it wasn't the same powerful tool it used to be and the right to petition evolved to be more like we think of it today: a collection of signatures in support of a cause or action.

Things Colonial Americans Petitioned For:

o Abolishing dueling, the practice of "gentlemen" hashing out arguments by shooting pistols at one another.

o Changing state lines. Massachusetts towns located on the border of Connecticut successfully petitioned Connecticut to accept them as part of its state borders (Massachusetts wasn't so happy about it).

o Sparing Black women from paying a required tax—just like white women. In 1769, a group of free Black men, some of mixed races, successfully petitioned for their wives and daughters to receive the same treatment as white women and not be required to pay Virginia's "head tax."

o Stopping illegal slave trade. By 1799, it was illegal to import people as slaves into the United States, but some illegal slave trade was happening with the country of Guinea. A group of seventy free Black men led by abolitionist Reverend Absalom Jones petitioned Congress to put a stop to it. In response, Congress passed a new law that doled out severe punishments for engaging in the forbidden trade.

·················· **GLOBAL PERSPECTIVE** ··················

CHINA

Although China's citizens do not have the same free speech rights as Americans, they do have a right to petition under a special system called *xinfang* that has existed for three thousand years! Under *xinfang*, Chinese citizens can bring up issues they have with the government and also private issues with individuals or companies. It's kind of like America's right to petition and judicial system rolled into one. *Xinfang* works side by side with China's court system. If someone files a lawsuit against someone else and loses, they still have the option to file a petition with a government bureau under *xinfang* and get that ruling overturned. It's like a last chance to be heard on an issue. Similar to the American petition system, numbers matter. The more petitioners that speak up about one issue, the more likely it will get noticed more quickly. But it's not the most effective system. Many people's petitions have toiled unresolved for years, even decades. Some even get inherited by sons and daughters after the petitioner has passed away.

Dear Mr. President

Whether it's by email or social media message or good old-fashioned snail mail, everyone has the right to send a direct message to the president! And not just the president, but any other public official like the vice president, your senator, your congresswoman, agency officials, or your state or local representatives. Kids in America have a long history of writing letters to the president. Sometimes presidents respond—and sometimes they even take action. It happened in 2016 when eight-year-old beauty pageant winner Mari Copeny decided to write a letter to then President Barack Obama about a gigantic problem her hometown of Flint, Michigan, was facing. Two years before, in order to save money, the state of Michigan had changed the source of Flint's drinking water. The problem was, the new source wasn't treated properly and the water that they drank, bathed in, washed their hands with, and used in cooking wasn't clean anymore. It was brown and it smelled funny. And that made people in Flint sick—some, really sick. People suspected the bad water was causing something called Legionnaire's disease, a respiratory illness that people died from. It was also connected to unpleasant problems like hair falling out and body rashes. To deal with this nasty, sickening water, Mari's family would drink bottled water and limit their showers to two minutes. They wanted to be clean, but they didn't want the shower water to make them sick. Mari and the rest of Flint believed their tap water should be free, clean, and safe like tap water in the rest of the country. Mari, along with her family and many townspeople, took to the streets in protest—using their First Amendment rights to assembly and free speech—to force the government to provide them with clean water. Mari wanted to do even more. She thought if she wrote to President Obama, maybe he would listen to her. She was Little Miss Flint, after all.

Mari wrote him a simple letter, containing just seven sentences, but it made a huge impact. She told President Obama she was traveling, along with many protesters from her town, to Washington, DC, to witness the congressional hearings where their governor had to answer questions about their contaminated water. Meeting him would lift peoples' spirits, Mari said. President Obama received Mari's letter, read it, and replied! He thanked her for writing and told her he was showing up to Flint, himself, where he would like to meet Mari and others to learn more about the serious problems they were facing.

The day he visited, she made sure to wear her purple Little Miss Flint sash. When it was her turn to shake hands with the president, she ran right up to him and he lifted her up in his arms. "You know, I wrote you!" she declared. "I know! That's why I decided to come!" President Barack Obama replied. After this meeting, a few months later, President Obama authorized $100 million to repair Flint's water system. Mari's advocacy didn't end with Flint's water crisis. She continues to help and be an activist for important issues like the Black Lives Matter movement. Mari hopes to run for president in 2044. "Obama was once a Black kid with a dream, and he was able to achieve it, so I can, too," she says. "When I'm president, I'll make sure I use my voice to speak for the people—especially kids."

How to Write a Letter to the President

Do you have an issue you really care about? Do you think the president of the United States should know about it? Do you have something you want to say to the president directly? Tell him! Or her, hopefully, one day soon! Kids can write a letter or send an email.

Want to write to a different public official? Check their website. Public officials will accept letters and often have ways to email them, even text them.

Tell the president what's on your mind and don't forget to tell the president something about yourself, too. Include your return address so you can get a letter back.

Here's a template to get you started:

[Your Address . . . important]

[Date]

President [First and last name]
The White House
1600 Pennsylvania Avenue
Washington, DC 20500

Dear Mr./Ms./Madame President,
[**WHO:** Introduce yourself! Talk about where you are from and important things about yourself you think the president should know, especially as it relates to your letter.]

[**WHAT:** State the reason for your letter. Explain why you are reaching out.]

[**WHY:** Explain why this is important to you and your community.]

[**HOW:** Describe just what the president can do to help you.]

[**THANKS:** Thank the president for reading your letter and helping out.]

Sincerely,

[Your name]
[Phone number]
[Email address]

Kids Harness the Power of the Petition

High school sophomore Sydney Helfand loved animals and was passionate about protecting them. To her, it made perfect sense to protect animals from horrible kinds of abuse. Didn't that make sense to everyone? Sydney believed animals deserved a federal law defending them from horrible human behavior. A bill called the Preventing Animal Cruelty and Torture Act (also known as PACT) proposed making it a federal crime to abuse animals. PACT had already been introduced to Congress, but it had failed to become a law. The Senate had approved the bill and it only needed to pass a vote by the House of Representatives, but a single congressperson had blocked having a vote on it at all. As a result, animals remained unprotected under federal law. This really bothered Sydney. Adults had failed to stand up for animals—could a kid help make it right? In January 2019, she opened her computer to the petition website Change.org and started her own petition to Congress, asking people to join her in showing their support of PACT, letting members of Congress know it was important to the American people to enact it into a law.

In her petition, Sydney explained what PACT was, why it was important, and how people could help. "The animals cannot speak for themselves. Please consider being the voice for the voiceless and sign the petition. Your support will speak volumes to lawmakers!" she said. She also suggested other ways people who cared about animals could help, including contacting their lawmakers directly and asking them to support the bill (an action that is also a First Amendment right under the Petition Clause!). She went live with her petition and it quickly drew the public's attention. As she gained more and more signatories, she provided updates on the status of the bill, action items on how people could further spread the word, and even uploaded a video where she spoke directly to the signatories. Her petition received over 860,000 signatures, including those of many kids and young people—a huge success. With so many Americans speaking up for animals, Congress couldn't ignore that passing PACT was the will of the people.

On January 31, 2019, PACT was reintroduced in Congress. The Senate and the House of Representative passed it with wide bipartisan support, meaning members of both the Republican and Democratic Parties voted to approve it. Sydney was invited to watch this historic moment that she had a hand in helping happen. On November 27, 2019, President Donald Trump signed PACT into law making it the first general federal animal cruelty law in US history. One of the bill's original sponsors, Representative Ted Deutsch, a Democrat from Florida, credited Sydney's petition with helping to successfully pass PACT so it became the law. The original creator of the bill and former head of the animal rights organization the Humane Society of the United States, Wayne Pacelle, also recognized Sydney's contribution: "Young people speak with a purity of intention that speaks to lawmakers."

CREATE A GREAT PETITION

Why should I start a petition?

Something has happened in the news or in your hometown or even to you or your friend or family member. You don't think it's right and you think someone in your local, state, or federal government can help make a difference in order to make it right. The subject of your petition should be something you feel really strongly about. Starting a petition to help this cause should make you feel like you are doing the right thing.

Who do you want to petition?

Think about who is in a position of power to help you. Maybe your issue has to do with something that affects your neighborhood in your hometown— the mayor or the town council might be the right people to petition. Perhaps it's an issue that affects a lot of people in your town and even beyond. In that case, your state representative or the congressperson who represents your district may be the right person. Or maybe it's something that you think the president of the United States should hear about. Or a federal agency that deals specifically with the kind of issue you are raising.

What resource do I use to start my petition?

Online petitions are easy to start thanks to petition websites like www .change.org and www.ipetitions.org.

The federal government also provides a way to petition it through its own website: petition.whitehouse.gov. Using this method, if your petition receives one hundred thousand signatures within thirty days, the White House is required to review your petition, which means policy experts read your petition, look into the issues you bring up, and provide an official response.

How do I get people to sign my petition?

The more signatures you have, the more powerful your petition is! Now you have to tell everyone about it! Talk about your petition to your family, your friends, your neighbors, your school community. Share your petition on social media and encourage others to do so, too. Think about what social media apps could have the biggest impact—perhaps TikTok or Twitter or Instagram. You could even contact your local newspaper or other news outlets about your petition. Think about what groups of people would be specifically interested in signing your petition and find a way to spread the word to them. Reach out to local lawmakers or influential people who may be interested in supporting your cause. Ask for help! Get your friends and family to help spread the word. Alert the person or body you are petitioning so they know you've started it.

Then what?

Keep your signatories informed of the progress of the petition and any updates that happen related to the issue you are petitioning about. Get creative!

What Should I Include in My Petition?

o **STATEMENT OF PURPOSE:** Explain why you are starting this petition.

o **INFORMATION ABOUT THE ISSUE:** Educate people on the issue. What exactly is it? Where is it occurring? Who is involved—are people being harmed? Who or what is responsible for harming others?

o **IDEAS ABOUT WHAT KINDS OF ACTION COULD MAKE A DIFFERENCE:** What are things the government can do to help? Perhaps it's passing a federal law or stopping an action that it is already doing.

o **REQUEST FOR SIGNATURES:** This is the key part! Make anyone signing your petition include their name and contact information so that their signature is verifiable.

o **OTHER WAYS PEOPLE CAN HELP:** Signing a petition is an easy way to help, but it's just a start. Suggest other things people can do to help, like contacting their local lawmakers or joining a protest.

SYDNEY HELFAND

Why were you drawn to use your right to petition?

I like to use my voice. I like to make changes in the world and if you can't use your voice, it's harder to make such an impact. I'm able to speak up and get people to speak up too—that's the cool thing about petitions. You put it out there for people to use their voice. It's letting other people use their voice too.

Had you ever done something like this before?

I did another petition on a much smaller scale for my middle school. I was this kid that wanted to make water bottles not allowed on campus. So I made a petition for that and the head of the school signed it. And now there are no water bottles on campus. It's just always been a thing for me and learning I can always make a difference with support and people.

What was your motivation to start your petition?

I was in my tenth-grade year. I just love animals. I love helping people. I like doing things. I knew before that this bill was blocked by one person in the Senate—which is crazy. I heard there was a new Democratic Congress. And this is the time, I knew I just needed to take action. So I created the petition.

How did you get started?

You have to know what it's about—the cause. And also—you have to believe in it yourself. I think that is the most important thing. That comes through when you write. I researched everything about the PACT Act and what it's all about. I tried to write the petition in a simple way so that people could really understand what I was saying. Really easy, so everyone could pop on, read it, and think: "Oh, this is a good thing"

How did you spread the word about your petition?

I went to different news sources. I talked on the radio and tried to spread it out to as many places as possible. Something that I actually learned that was really important was using technology in order to spread the message because that's the way of our time. Everyone uses technology. So I went on Facebook and I joined Facebook groups and I just spread the word. I spread the petition to lots of different areas to maximize its exposure. Pushing it out to groups, especially groups who believe in it. For my petition, I went to animal expos and stood there and asked people to sign it. I learned a lot through that process too. Going up to someone and asking "can you sign this?" It takes work and practice. At first people were just like "no" and just left. I got slightly better and more concise. I was not concise at first. At school, I went class to class and had a big group of people who supported this and helped me. Then, they would spread it out to their communities to maximize the exposure. I emailed Congressman Deutch as he was the original co-sponsor of the bill. We were communicating before and throughout most of this process. I did it all, so I can't really judge which was best. They are all important.

What was a highlight of this experience?

In July 2019, I spoke at Congress. Congressman Deutch invited me to help market the petition to the members of Congress. I spoke about the petition and how many signatures we got, which was the best experience of my life. It was just a really cool experience. I felt like I was really doing something for the world.

The day you went to speak before Congress, what was that like?

The most interesting day. Actually, I was not in this country. I was in Europe. I was doing a summer program, and then I found out I was asked to speak before Congress. I was like—I need to go home and I need to do this. So I flew by myself on the plane. I pulled basically an all-nighter and I wrote the speech on the plane on the way there and practiced. I went there straight from the airport and changed in the car. It was a whirlwind. It was amazing. I was really just excited. And I met so many people—the head of the Humane Society was there and a lot of other congresspeople. I was just really excited to be there and we were all here for a cause and it was amazing. I was actually delivering the signatures to Nancy Pelosi's office. I spoke and then I went in to deliver the petition. It was exciting! When you are there, you feel it. You feel, like, the place and how amazing it is. It feels like you are really making a difference just standing there.

What would you say are the major things you learned?

I think it is important and it's something that I have learned throughout my life—that no matter how old you are, no matter your background or what you do, you can still make a difference. And if you just set your mind to it, make it like: "I need to do this." And have a reason and make it a "must" to do it, then you can find a way to make a difference.

Kids vs. the United States of America

The Petition Clause allows Americans to file lawsuits against the government and have their cases reviewed by judges. Adults aren't the only people who can file a lawsuit. Kids can too! The mere act of filing a lawsuit makes a statement.

In 2015, a group of twenty-one young people, their ages ranging from eight to nineteen, decided they wanted to make a big statement about a big issue—the *biggest* issue: climate change. They filed a suit against the federal government, naming then President Barack Obama, the Office of the President, and several federal agencies, including the Environmental Protection Agency, the Department of Energy, and the Department of Agriculture, as defendants. They claimed that the adults in charge were ruining the environment that kids were going to inherit and that was seriously unfair. The impact of climate change was dire and America needed to reduce carbon emissions and stop its reliance on fossil fuels, like, yesterday.

According to the kids, the federal government was infringing on their constitutional right to a clean environment. This case, known as *Juliana v. United States of America*, was the first of its kind and this group of bold young activists made headlines across the globe.

The group included boys and girls from all over the country. Among them was eighteen-year-old Alexander Loznak, whose 570-acre family farm in Kellogg, Oregon, had deeply felt the impact of climate change. Levi D. from Satellite Beach, Florida, was the youngest plaintiff at just eight years old. The barrier island he called home had been battered by the increased number of hurricanes caused by climate change. Fifteen-year-old Xiuhtezcatl Tonatiuh Martinez from Boulder, Colorado, was raised in the Aztec tradition with a deep respect for nature. So deep, that he founded an activist group called the Earth Guardians. An adult climate change scientist also joined the group of kid plaintiffs.

With their lawsuit, the kids hoped that a judge would decide in their favor and require the government to take action by implementing a science-based plan to reduce carbon emissions and eliminate fossil fuels. They knew a victory was a longshot and they probably wouldn't win, but they also knew that just by exercising their right to petition in filing this lawsuit, the world's eyes and ears would be focused on them and their message: something big must be done to combat climate change *now*.

Even though the Obama White House probably was proud of the kids for taking a stand and even though some of the defendants probably agreed that the government could be doing a better job, making the changes the kids wanted was a huge deal and would be really hard to accomplish. The Obama White House believed these kinds of big decisions were best made by Congress or the White House itself—not by a judge. The White House's motivation to defend itself got even stronger after Donald Trump was elected and his administration took over the case. The Trump administration was less interested in combating climate change and was ready to fight the lawsuit.

Juliana v. United States of America was taken seriously from the beginning. The first judge in the district court ruled that the kids had put together a compelling case and should be allowed to proceed. This made the fossil fuel industry really nervous. All of this made international news, covered by major news outlets like the *New York Times*, the *Wall Street Journal*, and CNN for years. Unfortunately, the kids faced defeat when a Ninth Circuit appeals court judge ruled against them. It was clear that Judge Andrew D. Hurwitz thought what the kids had done was amazing, that the threat of climate change was real, and that they had "made a compelling case that action is needed." But Judge Hurwitz agreed with the government—taking the kinds of actions to combat climate change should be done by Congress or the president, not through the court system and this lawsuit. The kids have filed another appeal and are awaiting a new decision—their fight isn't over.

Although Alexander, Levi, Xiuhtezcatl, and their co-plaintiffs didn't get the outcome they hoped for in court, their lawsuit was a success in other ways. Their bold use of their right to petition inspired other kids who were demanding more action against climate change to file lawsuits against their state governments. They also inspired sixteen young people from across the globe, including environmental activist Greta Thunberg, to file a lawsuit in the United Nations stating that the world's worst offenders of creating greenhouse gases were violating an international agreement called the Convention on the Rights of the Child. Thanks to the kid plaintiffs of *Juliana v. United States of America*, an army of kids around the world continue to fight for their rights to a clean environment using their right to petition.

Right to Petition Tools: Which Should I Use?

TOOL	WHAT IT IS	UPSIDE	DOWNSIDE
PETITION	Collection of signatures in support of an issue or request	o Many voices joined together can make a big impact o It's free to start one o Informs many people about the issue o Large number of signatories can potentially attract media attention	o It's hard to collect a lot of signatures. You need 100,000 to be reviewed by the US government o May go unanswered
LETTER TO PRESIDENT	Personal letter to the president of the United States	o It's free or the cost of a postage stamp o It's more personal—you can use your voice to say just what you want in the way you want to	o A single voice may not be as powerful as many joined together o May go unanswered
LAWSUIT	Legal court action	o Government is required to respond in court o If you win, a decision is final and can require the government to make the change you want o Can attract media attention and spread your message to a lot of people	o It's very expensive o Can go on for a long time, often years o You might lose!

The Power of Knowing Your Rights

Congratulations! You now know a whole lot about your First Amendment freedoms guaranteed by the US Constitution! And guess what? You didn't need a law degree. These rights belong to EVERYONE. They always have and always will.

Now that you know you have the right to freely practice (or not practice) your religion, the rights to free speech, a free press, to freely assemble, and to petition the government, you have the power to PROTECT these rights.

Just by knowing your rights, you are more likely to use them. Maybe that means joining a protest for a cause you believe in; writing a letter to the president asking for change; becoming an editor of your school paper; or proudly wearing a religious symbol to school or wearing a hairstyle that reflects your culture. Maybe you will just go about your normal life, but now you'll have the deep satisfaction of recognizing when you are lucky enough to be using those precious American freedoms.

You're now a part of the longstanding tradition of kids in America standing up for their First Amendments rights. You're now charged with the mission to protect those rights. You're more certain to know when those rights are being threatened, attacked, or just plain ripped away. You're much more aware of how/when/where/why to use those epic rights with purpose. And you're likely more eager to ensure your First Amendment rights are fully respected while the rights of your classmates, friends, and fellow citizens are also upheld. Last, but not least, you now know those rights empower you to be who you are and all that you can be.

Acknowledgments

We would like to thank our literary agent Lilly Ghahremani for her relentless dedication, focused vision, diligence, friendship—all the things! We also greatly appreciate Stefanie Sanchez Von Borstel and the rest of the fabulous team at Full Circle Literary.

Many thanks to the whole team at Running Press Kids, especially our dynamic editor, Allison Cohen, who leaned into our mission to empower children to know their First Amendment rights. Special thanks to RPK's Frances J. Soo Ping Chow, the designer; Amber Morris, the production editor; Rebecca Matheson and Kara Thornton, in charge of marketing/publicity; and the rest of the team who helped bring our vision to life.

Thank you to Mary Beth Tinker, Jerome Foster II, Sydney Helfand, and all children who have taken or inspired action to secure the rights of our youngest citizens. Your courage and tenacity take our breath away.

ALLISON MATULLI would like to thank her loved ones, students, teachers, colleagues, and fellow social engineers for never giving up on the brilliant ambition of children to seek knowledge needed, sound the alarm for human equality, and expect universal kindness. Thank you to social justice pioneer Melba V. Pearson, law school mentor Galen Medley, and Howard University School of Law for mentoring her love of law. She would like to thank a man who she met over twenty years ago, in the historic center of picturesque downtown Rome, Italy, in one of those fairytale boy-meets-girl stories. His name is Gianluca, and as her husband and life partner, he has supported Allison to fly higher beyond the moon and dance on the stars. As they say in Italy, *"Grazie amore mio!"* Allison also wishes to share a heartfelt thank-you with her son, Santo Max, and daughter, Eva Skye, whose life experiences as multiethnic, bilingual, first-generation American kids ignite her need to use storytelling and books to empower the next generation. Santo Max and Eva Skye, you are a dream realized. Last, but not least, Allison wants to thank her brother, Bevin, who has always eagerly walked this lifelong road as her true friend.

CLELIA CASTRO-MALASPINA would like to thank her friends, family, colleagues, and loved ones for all of their support. She must single out her husband, Michael, who has never wavered in his belief in her and has always encouraged her to pursue everything she's passionate about. How very lucky she is to have him as her partner in life. She'd like to acknowledge her parents, who encouraged her to pursue a law career, and kindly supported her decision to leave that career—hopefully the writing of this book makes you proud. Special thanks to her law school friends, professors, and former law firm colleagues for helping instill a respect, appreciation, and love of law. Finally, Clelia would like to thank her daughters, Azalea and Samantha, who continuously inspire Clelia to strive to be the best version of herself.

Selected Sources

LAWS

US Constitution. Amendment I.

BOOKS

Bartoletti, Susan Campbell. *Kids on Strike!* Boston: Houghton Mifflin Harcourt, 1999.

Berkin, Carol. *The Bill of Rights: The Fight to Secure America's Liberties.* New York: Simon & Schuster, 2016.

Demuth, Patricia Brennan. *What Is the Constitution?* New York: Penguin Workshop, 2018.

Dierenfield, Bruce J. *The Battle over School Prayer: How Engel v. Vitale Changed America.* Lawrence: University Press of Kansas, 2007.

Driver, Justin. *The School-House Gate: Public Education, the Supreme Court, and the Battle for the American Mind.* New York: Vintage Books, 2018.

Ellis, Richard J. *To the Flag: The Unlikely History of the Pledge of Allegiance.* Lawrence: University Press of Kansas, 2005.

Henderson, Leah. *Together We March: 25 Protest Movements That Marched into History.* New York: Atheneum, 2021.

Hudson, David L., Jr. *Let the Students Speak!: A History of the Fight for Free Expression in American Schools.* Boston: Beacon Press, 2011.

Levinson, Cynthia. *The Youngest Marcher: The Story of Audrey Fay Hendricks, a Young Civil Rights Activist.* New York: Atheneum, 2017.

Long, Michael G. *Kids on the March: 15 Stories of Speaking Out, Protesting, and Fighting for Justice.* New York: Algonquin, 2021.

Olivas, Michael A., and Ronna Greff Schneider, eds. *Education Law Stories.* New York: Foundation Press, 2009.

Pimental, Annette Bay. *All the Way to the Top: How One Girl's Fight for Americans with Disabilities Changed Everything.* Chicago: Sourcebooks, 2020.

WEBSITES

American Civil Liberties Union (ACLU). "Free Speech." Issues tab. https://www.aclu.org/issues/free-speech.

———. "Know Your Rights: Protesters' Rights." https://www.aclu.org /know-your-rights/protesters-rights/?redirect=free-speech%2Fknow -your-rights-demonstrations-and-protests&utm_source=pocket_mylist.

American Library Association (ALA). "Top Ten Most Challenged Books List." Banned & Challenged Books. https://www.ala.org/advocacy/bbooks /frequentlychallengedbooks/top10

Cope, Sophia, and Adam Schwartz. "You Have a First Amendment Right to Record the Police." Electronic Frontier Foundation, June 8, 2020. https://www.eff.org/deeplinks/2020/06/you-have-first-amendment -right-record-police.

Hinduja, Sameer, and Justin W. Patchin. "State Bullying Laws." Cyberbullying Research Center. Updated January 2021. https://cyberbullying.org /Bullying-and-Cyberbullying-Laws.pdf.

National Coalition Against Censorship. "First Amendment Rights for Student Protesters." 2017. https://ncac.org/wp-content/uploads/2017/11/Student -Protest-Rights.pdf.

Pew Research Center. "For a Lot of American Teens, Religion Is a Regular Part of the Public School Day." October 3, 2019. https://pewresearch.org /religion/2019/10/03/for-a-lot-of-american-teens-religion-is-a-regular -part-of-the-public-school-day/.

Student Press Law Center. "Fighting Censorship After Hazelwood." November 6, 2015. https://splc.org/2015/11/fighting-censorship -after-hazelwood/.

Supreme Court of the United States. "The Supreme Court at Work." https://www.supremecourt.gov/about/courtatwork.aspx.

The White House. "How You Can Write or Call the White House." https://www.whitehouse.gov/get-involved/write-or-call/.

———. "The Judicial Branch." https://www.whitehouse.gov /about-the-white-house/our-government/the-judicial-branch/.

SUPREME COURT CASES

Board of Education, Island Trees Union Free School District No. 26 v. Pico by Pico, 457 U.S. 853 (1982). https://www.oyez.org/cases/1981/80-2043.

Board of Education of Westside Community Schools v. Mergens By and Through Mergens, 496 U.S. 226 (1990). https://www.oyez.org /cases/1989/88-1597.

Engel v. Vitale, 370 U.S. 421 (1962). https://www.oyez.org/cases/1961/468.

Epperson v. Arkansas, 393 U.S. 97 (1968). https://www.oyez.org/cases/1968/7.

Hazelwood School District v. Kuhlmeier, 484 U.S. 260 (1988). https://www.oyez.org/cases/1987/86-836.

Lee v. Weisman, 505 U.S. 577 (1992). https://www.oyez.org/cases/1991/90-1014.

Mahanoy Area School District v. B. L., 594 U.S. __ (2021). https://www.oyez.org/cases/2020/20-255.

Minersville School District v. Gobitis, 310 U.S. 586 (1940). https://www.oyez.org/cases/1940-1955/310us586.

Tinker v. Des Moines Independent Community School District, 393 U.S. 503 (1969). https://www.oyez.org/cases/1968/21.

West Virginia State Board of Education v. Barnette, 319 U.S. 624 (1943). https://www.oyez.org/cases/1940-1955/319us624.

Did You Know?

Did you know it can take up to 18 months to write and publish a book? That means that while this book went to press, some of the cases and examples highlighted in this book have seen developments. History is ever-changing, so one of the best ways to stay informed is to watch/read/listen to the news, do your research, and stay current on events happening in our nation.

About the Authors

Allison Matulli is a former attorney and educator, now founder and dean of legal literacy for The Little Lawyers and adjunct professor at FIU's department of Criminology and Criminal Justice. Allison is an educational reform activist dedicated to making sure kids know their constitutional rights, which is a focal point of *Your Freedom, Your Power*. She is also the author of *I Am Because We Are*, a picture book about the responsibility to community. Additionally, Allison leads workshops and clinics and is a speaker on issues regarding race, systemic racism, prejudice, legal literacy, diversity, and inclusion. Formerly a teacher at independent schools (where she was lovingly known as "Professor Ally") and a certified American Montessori Society lead educator, she has always worked to incorporate legal literacy into her classroom. When she could not find the vital tools she needed to do so, she created her own.

The Little Lawyers is an organization that excites and empowers children to learn the law. Today, its curriculum products for school and home-based learning are used throughout Miami-Dade County, the fourth largest school district in the country, and in several other major cities (e.g., Houston, San Francisco, Las Vegas, Philadelphia, and New York), with over 17,000 students having participated in the program through local workshops, educational materials, and more. Allison has seen firsthand the transformation that happens when children are empowered by their understanding of the law, and it's her biggest dream to impact children in this way and on the largest scale possible.

Allison continues to use her voice to speak up for children's rights and has been a keynote speaker for Black Voices at the Miami Beach Woman's Club, FIU's Miami Black Womxn's Forum, and Tuesday Times (a round-table sponsored by *The New York Times*). Allison holds a BA in economics from St. Joseph's University, a master's in education from Endicott College, and a juris doctorate from Howard University School of Law. She is based in Miami where she lives with her husband and two children, Santo Max and Eva Skye. You can learn more about Allison at www.thelittlelawyers.com.

 **Clelia Castro-Malaspina** is a former attorney and literary agent and works as a freelance writer and developmental editor of children's books at Mossy Pines Creative. She is dedicated to bringing diverse, meaningful, and illuminating books to the next generations. As an agent, she worked with award-winning, bestselling, and acclaimed fiction and nonfiction writers. As a lawyer, she practiced as a litigator at an international corporate law firm and then a boutique law practice specializing in public criminal defense under the Criminal Justice Act for indigent federal defendants. Although she is no longer a practicing attorney, she has remained legal-minded and shares Allison's goal to make the law more accessible to kids. She received her bachelor's degrees in English and communications from Boston College, her law degree from American University Washington College of Law and her master's in publishing and writing from Emerson College. She currently lives with her husband and two daughters in Mercer Island, Washington. You can read more about Clelia at www.mossypinescreative.com.